THE LEADERSHIP LESSONS OF HOWARD STERN

June 2024

Dear JD, Aviana, Mila, Carla & Eva

Thank you for being such great leaders in my life.

We've only just begun

With love

HOW THE KING OF ALL MEDIA
CAN MAKE US BETTER LEADERS

THE
LEADERSHIP LESSONS
OF
HOWARD STERN

AN UNAUTHORIZED GUIDEBOOK

Michael W. Kublin
PRESIDENT, PEOPLETEK, INC.
DBA PEOPLETEK COACHING
(ALL RIGHTS RESERVED)

Copyright © 2023 by Michael W. Kublin

All rights reserved. No part of this book may be used or reproduced in any manner whatsoever without prior written consent of the author, except as provided by the United States of America copyright law.

Published by Best Seller Publishing®, St. Augustine, FL
Best Seller Publishing® is a registered trademark.
Printed in the United States of America.

ISBN: 978-1-959840-83-1

Disclaimer: Howard Stern had absolutely no involvement in the creation of this publication. This book was not authorized by him.

This publication is designed to provide accurate and authoritative information with regard to the subject matter covered. It is sold with the understanding that the publisher is not engaged in rendering legal, accounting, or other professional advice. If legal advice or other expert assistance is required, the services of a competent professional should be sought. The opinions expressed by the author in this book are not endorsed by Best Seller Publishing® and are the sole responsibility of the author rendering the opinion.

For more information, please write:
Best Seller Publishing®
1775 US-1 #1070
St. Augustine, FL 32084
or call 1 (626) 765-9750
Visit us online at: www.BestSellerPublishing.org

Contents

Dedication 1
A Little About PeopleTek and The Leadership COMPASS 5
Preface 17
Introduction: Personal Accountability 27
1   A Better Leader Now (Where Howard and PeopleTek's Leadership COMPASS Meet) 37
2   The Importance of Self-Awareness and CourageAbility 53
3   Magic Dust 71
4   Vision, Mission, Goals, Measures = Behavior 85
5   Communication and Listening 101
6   Clarity 109
7   Accountability 117
8   Conflict (Without Conflict There Is No Leadership) 123
9   Influence 129
10 Relationships 137
11 Feedback 143
12 Inspiration 149
13 Continual Learning 157
14 Action Steps 163
Howard Stern: Setting PeopleTek Standards Since His Beginning 167
Epilogue 173
About the Author 177

Dedication

This book is dedicated to my father, Alvin (Big Al) Kublin. I asked my father prior to his 90th birthday in 2019 how he always greeted everyone positively and was so upbeat. This was especially remarkable because he was in a terrible car accident in 2002 where he lost his arm and leg and became paralyzed, and he hadn't walked since then. He said simply, *I made a decision*. I said, *What do you mean, you made a decision? Is that a spiritual thing?* He said, *No, I made a decision that no person or any situation was going to make me angry, sad, or worried again*.

I never realized how powerful decisions can be in making us happier people and better leaders. That decision process helped me greatly from that day forward in so many areas of my life. Thank you to Dad, for helping me, and for leaving this world better than you found it.

My hopes are that you decide right now to learn and grow as a leader. By deciding now to read and do the exercises in this book, you and many others will make this a better, more responsible planet of great leaders.

*My dad, Big Al (front row center), my mom,
Phyllis Kublin (on right), Dad's aide, Jean Augustine
(next to Dad on left), my son, Harrison Kublin (on left),
my nephew, Myles (on right), and me (back center)*

A Little About PeopleTek and The Leadership COMPASS

I have a major hope for everyone who wishes to be a better leader. We are all leaders. Every person on the planet is a leader and is very special. Many will dispute this, and that is fine; go right ahead and waste your time.

For over 25 years, PeopleTek has been developing leaders who can be proud of all they accomplish and who live their careers with passion and joy — and in alignment with a greater purpose. From the time I was first in a leadership role until a few years after I was promoted to a higher level position, I was never given the tools and processes in order to be the greatest leader I could. Basically, the formula was to learn from others before you; take a class; or, if a little more advanced, implement things learned from life experiences like the military or religious organizations. Some people even had mentors. Coaches at that time were few to nonexistent.

When I dropped out of corporate America to start my Coaching and Leadership Company, and after several years of working as an Executive Coach, I noticed a trend. A lot of people were a lot like me. They were good at doing a job or task, got promoted into leadership, and no one ever gave them a process to be the best leaders they could. Now, many companies have leadership training, development, and coaching programs; however, they are not totally aligned with helping the leaders succeed and truly live with established vision, missions, goals, measures, values, and behavior.

Most companies, when asked, say our most valuable asset is our people. Do they really live that based on behavior and actions they demonstrate or do they just say it with words? It's easy to say something in writing or put it in words on a wall. What's harder to do is live it. If we truly believe in people, then we need to behave that way at all levels and prove it in all our processes. That is why I created the Leadership Journey Program.

I want to provide everyone at all levels with the tools and insights to be a great leader in any position. I believe that all of us are leaders, no matter what our title or level. To this end, I developed the Leadership COMPASS, which follows the curriculum of the Leadership Journey Program.

The COMPASS provides an overview for leaders of the tools they need in order to be successful and live their careers in alignment with their values and beliefs. Take your time and look at each area of the COMPASS and begin a process to build your leadership muscles. Not only will you enjoy your career, have more engagement, and effectively lead others, you will leave this planet a better place than you found it.

Here are the twelve areas of the Leadership COMPASS.

1. Self-Awareness — We must look inside to see how we "show up" to others. We must also look at how we see ourselves, and what beliefs, behaviors, and values we

live by. This area involves asking ourselves a series of questions and finding out answers by digging deeply into our thoughts, feelings, actions, and values. We need to look at what we want and what we don't want. How we handle conflict, change, decision-making, planning, structure, order, analysis, empathy, and many other issues. This takes vulnerability (being open and receptive). It requires receiving feedback and using assessments such as Myers-Briggs, DiSC, Enneagram, Hogan, StrengthsFinder, TKI, Team Dimensions, EQ-i 2.0 (Emotional Quotient Inventory), and numerous other techniques of self-discovery. We must investigate to uncover our blind spots, acknowledge our strengths, and learn how we may at times overuse them or let them get in our way. The bottom line is we must know where we are now and where we want or need to go for our future state. Your journey starts with Self-Awareness.

2. Magic Dust — What are my skills, abilities, and talents that make me special? We all have Magic Dust. We are all special. It is important to find out why and how to describe it, and to understand how it works. We may be great at certain things, and others may be great at what they do. Magic Dust usually comes easy to us, and we don't understand why others can't do it that way. This magic comes from our strengths and areas of behavior that come so easily to us that sometimes we don't recognize them. We need to examine past assignments, roles, responsibilities, and what we liked and didn't like. We need to honor ourselves to be able to discuss our Magic Dust in an instant. We need to honor others and respect each person on the planet for theirs. We need

to advertise our Magic Dust, communicate about it, and not be afraid to share it with others. It should be the first thing on our résumé.

3. Vision, Mission, Goals, Measures = Behaviors — What is it we are trying to achieve, and why? Does this align with our values and actions? Does this (career, business, life plan, or the like) align with our behavior? This plan should guide our behavior, including what we spend our money and time on, how we educate ourselves, where we have fun, and how we live. Everything we do should align with our vision, mission, goals, and measures. We must have a plan as leaders. We are all leaders; therefore, we should all have a plan that is documented, reviewed, and updated as required. If we don't have one now, we must develop one and not be afraid to write it down, then make changes if necessary. When asked, we need to be able to produce our plan right away.

4. Communication — Do we communicate with all others in a healthy, honoring, respectful manner no matter who they are or what they look like? Do we honor their Magic Dust and respect them for it? Do we speak to others in their style and not think everyone is like us? Are they introverted, extroverted, domineering, friendly, social, empathic? The point is that all these things and many more influence our communication with others.

5. Clarity — We need a process to get us aligned so that we carry out our vision, mission, and goals, and execute best practices and processes in our approach. There are various roles we play, so clarity needs to be understood

in everything we do as an individual for our career, our team, or our organization. For example:

- Individual — What work do we align with, and what role do we play? How do we invest our money? What coaches or mentors are aligned with our vision, dreams, and goals?
- Team — Who gets to be on our team, and what values do they live by? How do we hire, reward, train, coach, and develop, and what processes are we responsible for?
- Organization — The same questions apply as those for a team, except they are aligned for the entire organization.

6. Accountability — We need to hold ourselves and others accountable for what was agreed. First, accountability begins with us, and then it is others. As John Miller, author of the book *QBQ!*, says, we must take responsibility and not pass the buck. We own it. We need to ask ourselves what we can do and how. Not who is to blame and why. We need to give ourselves feedback without beating ourselves up. This is not easy because at times we are so very hard on ourselves. We need to be rational about our expectations of ourselves and at the same time move forward toward our vision, mission, and goals. The measures and behaviors reflect our accountability and progress. When we lead a team, the measures are the team's, and in turn, the organization's. They give us a way to determine whether we're moving forward appropriately. Do we need to change anything guiding us? Our measures are a checkpoint to ensure our

behavior is appropriate and in alignment with where we said we desire to go with our vision, mission, and goals.

7. Conflict — There will be conflict. Do we know and understand how we show up so we can handle conflict in a healthy, honoring, and respectful manner? Conflict is uncomfortable. It is hard for a lot of people. When we hold ourselves accountable, it is uncomfortable. When we hold others accountable, it is also uncomfortable. If you are not empowering yourself and others to go where they've never gone before, then everything is too status quo. You must encourage yourself and others to do better, learn more, grow, and develop. There is a saying we must live by: Without Conflict, There Is No Leadership. We need to ask whether we are having healthy conflict for ourselves and others.

8. Influence — Are our vision, mission, goals, and measures clear? Do others understand what is expected of them to succeed with us as leaders helping leaders? We all must understand how we are coming across. Are we being too passive? Are we being too aggressive? Influence can be exerted by taking actions that carry out our established vision, mission, and goals. Too often, we think aligning our vision, mission, and goals with others needs to be hard work and forced, when in fact we are influencing just by doing things and letting others see and hear about what we are doing. How much relationship behavior and task behavior do we have? Do we need more? As the Thomas-Kilmann conflict mode Instrument (TKI) shows us, we need to understand what mode to use and when to influence in the appropriate manner.

9. Relationships — We need to recognize the importance of internal and external relationships, and how they impact our ability to achieve our short- and long-term goals. Our relationships are the only thing that will be remembered years down the line. Who are you meeting with? When? What groups are you involved with? Do they relate to your vision, mission, and goals? Do those groups know what your vision, mission, and goals are? Can others feel a bond with you? Everyone you meet is an important person, and it is very good to understand you are meeting them for a reason. The things you will remember most in all your work and assignments are the relationships you make along the way.

10. Feedback — Can we be vulnerable enough to receive it? Feedback is something that can benefit us greatly if and when we are open to receiving it. There are things that others can easily see about us that we can't see right away. These include our strengths, development areas, fears, and aspirations, among many other things. Once we receive the feedback, we can decide whether we want to make those changes and accept what is being told to us, or whether we want to file the feedback away. There is no right or wrong answer. Many of us think we have to make the changes and therefore become afraid of receiving feedback. This is not true. We don't have to accept one word of it. We can look at our values, vision, mission, and goals and see how — if at all — the feedback ties in. The key is to be receptive and to listen. Can anyone come to us and have us listen without judgment to their issue? Listening doesn't mean anything needs to be done — that is always up to you!

11. Inspiration — This is something that either comes internally or can be a spark from someone or something external to us. It can be input that suddenly got us to make a change, or it can be from a long-term process of self-reflection. Ultimately it is up to us to make the changes; however, by our changing, we can help others change as well. The motivation can come from words in a book or a speech, from TV or the news, or from our values, dreams, and aspirations. What will drive us toward our plans? We are all leaders. But how do we get ourselves to show up? It is ultimately up to each of us. Someone may cause us to make that change; and we can be very grateful and open to hearing stories from others about how they build their inspiration and motivation for what they want to accomplish in their careers and life. How do we inspire others to understand they are emerging leaders? How do we help and coach others to be successful? We are all in this together, and we all need one another's help.

12. Continual Leadership Learning — I think this is a very important part of Leadership Learning because it says, as a leader, my responsibility to gain more knowledge and expertise is never done. This means that Leadership Learning is a process and not an event. Just like we go to a gym to build our physical strength, we must do the same for our leadership skills. We have to understand we will be tested to use these muscles all the time, so we need to understand how we show up when we are using them in real time. How we approach our vision, mission, goals, and measures and how we guide others to be inspired toward a common goal requires many

disciplines. There are so many paths that can be taken, and it is up to each of us as individuals to ensure we have done all we can to be successful. This might mean occasionally falling down as we practice these principles every day. Remember to consider what our style of communication is and whether we are speaking to others who are different from us. What is the best way to handle conflict for the specific situation we are in? Do we manage change in our team with various forms of empathy? How do we hold ourselves and others accountable? These are lifelong habits, and as we move forward with various roles and responsibilities, we need to use different techniques to handle those who are looking to us as guides for their careers. Even if we are not officially their boss, others are looking at how we show up. We need to take ownership and responsibility so that we show up in the best way possible. This is not only for now but forever.

THE PURPOSES OF THIS BOOK

This book is for everyone who wants to be a better leader for the sake of themselves, their career, and the companies they serve or own — now and in the future.

In the interest of simplifying the traits contained within the Leadership COMPASS, this book will lay out three main areas of Leadership that will be covered:

1. Magic Dust Congruency and Community

2. Authentic Confidence in the Face of External/Internal Conflict

3. Self-Determined Awareness and Development

For too many of us, this information is not apparent or laid out so that we can begin a process of building our skills, abilities, and talents in these areas. Our Magic Dust is defined as our special, unique skills and abilities that make us thrive and feel joy when we are using them. Respecting and honoring every other person's Magic Dust is crucial. We cannot achieve greatness without the Magic Dust of others.

If we are appropriately living our Magic Dust daily and allowing others to help and serve us with theirs, then we and they will all be more successful in achieving our determined vision, mission, and goals. Our dreams and aspirations are very personal, almost impossible to achieve, and eternal (the dream lives forever). If you are in congruence with living your life daily by sharing your Magic Dust and vision, mission, and goals, then communication, conflict resolution, and long-lasting relationships come naturally.

We are encouraging others to live their Magic Dust and live in congruence with their own goals and desires. There is no strain because everything becomes authentic when both internal and external forces of life are thrust upon us and our careers. The approach we must take is to be driven internally by our own self-motivation. I like to look at my Magic Dust as the initial spark and inspiration for others to make changes in order to live a more joyous and prosperous career and life. After that spark, it is up to you to take it from there.

Self-determination, continued development, and learning through awareness are musts. To be truly accountable means that we are the leaders of our lives, careers, and destiny, and we don't just survive — we live. I like Oscar Wilde's quote that says, "To live is the rarest thing in the world. Most people exist, that is all." When you think about it, this is sad. But why is this quotation true? Because we minimize our power and greatness.

For many years, when I didn't understand or know what Magic Dust or Vision, Mission, and Goals were, I took roles and made career decisions that did not suit me well. I knew many others who did the same thing: they took a job or role because it was offered to them. This time does not go totally to waste, since it provides us with many great opportunities and insights. Yet, we cause our own sadness or dissatisfaction because we don't make changes we need that align better with who we are and what we are all about. This is because we made the decision and also because of money or other factors of life. I stayed for many years, seventeen, before I started to make these career choices. Many others I know never decided and waited each day for retirement. I don't want those reading this book to do the same. I want you to empower yourself now to move forward and make some hard but very valuable decisions with the information you discover along this Journey.

We live small. I want everyone who is reading this to begin to live big, like the very special and unique individuals and leaders we all are.

Preface

I am so very excited because today in our team meeting, one of the members said that Howard was recognized on MSNBC as being one of the best interviewers ever. Several other members said, "Ooh, Howard Stern, he is so very crude, and Mike should not be writing about him as a leader."

This made me so happy. Why? Because that is the entire point. We all have strengths and areas to develop. In 30-plus years of doing this work, I haven't met anyone yet at any level who doesn't have areas to develop. While I've never met him personally, as a fan, I've enjoyed how Howard has grown and transformed his behavior over the years. This book will demonstrate how each of us needs to look inside at our own strengths and determine how we may overuse them and let them get in our way. The other reason I am pleased about their response is that it didn't influence me to stop writing. In fact, I kept going. For too long as a leader, I wanted other people to offer confirmation on what I should do. I wanted their approval. One of the main concepts of this book is that others' approval doesn't matter. No one's except my own does. I want you to believe and act the same way. Many of us seek the approval of others.

We seek approval from family members, clergy, friends, business associates, and so on. They want to give us their best advice and have no ill intention — they want to protect us. This protection can keep us from attaining our vision, mission, and goals, and our life and career dreams. These people want to protect us from failing or even feeling bad and getting hurt. But you cannot grow and transform unless you take a risk. I want you to do that as you read this book. Howard did so in his life, and I know for sure he had many people telling him he would fail. Thank goodness he didn't listen to them.

A few years before I wrote this book you're now holding, I was initially going to send Howard a draft copy of my book but kept delaying. Several months passed; then my fiancée, Wilda, bought me a copy of Howard's newest book, *Howard Stern Comes Again*, for my birthday. She knows how much I respect him, for so many reasons. I had told her about my Leadership Lessons of Howard Stern idea and that I wanted to create a book about using PeopleTek's Leadership Journey Program and Journey COMPASS. The COMPASS includes twelve foundational categories, and the journey is all about self-reflection for leaders. The overall goal is to lead people more effectively in a way that aligns with whatever the leader or team members do best.

After reading Howard's book and learning more about what he included, I came to the realization, and agreed with Howard, that this book was 100 percent better than any of his previous books.

I'd read his past books, and they were clearly not at the level of quality and depth of this masterpiece. His past books were amateurish compared to what he had released this time. In each interview, there is deep, meaningful content, which provides the reader insights that demonstrate Howard's continual leadership, learning, and development. Thus, the book further proves why he is one of the greatest leaders and coaches of our time. He gives us a glimpse into why we can all lead a better, more joyous life, and proves that learning is a lifelong process that begins with deep self-reflection. Howard said, "It's my best book of them all," and I totally agree.

I am so glad that I never got a chance to send Howard the first draft of my book, which I had been planning to mail earlier. At the time, I thought I had explored my ideas with depth and clarity. Looking back, my instinct is that sending him my book would have resulted in a collision, not a culmination. In addition, Howard himself, in on-air interviews, is totally open about how his work with a counselor has helped him be more effective. Previously, he'd thought he had to behave in a certain way and that he didn't need to with his interview style. He could still be the greatest and not alienate his guests. He points this out with some interviews, like one with Robin Williams in which Howard could have decided to use a different approach. It's strange how the world works with our timing and goals.

Howard empowers us to go where we've never gone before and does this with finesse and kindness. He is a true lifelong leadership learner, as proven by the fact that he now uses finesse with his interviews way more than he used to. He said recently that he can have even more impact doing what he does in a nice way, like he does now, than before when he had little empathy for those he was interviewing. He admitted he likes this new approach.

So, you may ask, Why Howard? Out of all the people in the world, why did I want to use Howard Stern to illustrate effective leadership?

Very few have a more polarizing public persona than does Howard. Howard has a reputation for being sexist, obnoxious, small-thinking — for being a nutty, outlandish person. The media has said that he may be losing his mojo. A *New York Post* article from April 2021[1] reads:

> Once upon a time, you could argue that would be fair compensation [the article refers to Stern's pay of $1 million per show]; after all, one could never predict what Stern would do or say. As memorialized by an analyst in Stern's 1997 biopic *Private Parts*:
>
> "The average radio listener listens for 18 minutes. The average Howard Stern fan listens for, are you ready for this, an hour and 20 minutes … Answer most commonly given? 'I want to see what he'll say next.'"
>
> As for those who loathed Stern: "The average Stern hater listens for two and a half hours a day … Most common answer? 'I want to see what he'll say next.'"
>
> Today, it's all too easy to predict what Stern will say next. Don't just take my word for it — endless Reddit threads and Facebook groups are devoted to carbon dating the show's death, parsing over its comedic breadcrumbs and wondering why Stern even bothers anymore.

---

[1] https://nypost.com/2021/04/27/howard-stern-has-lost-his-sting-and-his-mojo/

Indeed, Stern sounds like a guy who should have retired years ago, one begging to be fired, an attempt to end his own misery.

Howard: Your listeners are right there with you. Put us all out of your misery.

Consider a typical show, consisting — on a daily, *Ground Day*-like basis — of such content as imitations of his nonagenarian parents and their hearing loss ("What?! What did you say?!") — as enjoyable as talking to one's own hard-of-hearing relatives — while revisiting slights and traumas from his childhood yet insisting that decades of three-to-four-day-a-week therapy have made him less angry and more evolved.

By Howard openly talking about going to therapy, he gives each of us "permission" to be vulnerable. This is crucial for a leader. He shows us his humanity. More leaders need to do this. The traditional "I am strong and have no issues" leader has been replaced by honest, truthful displays of reality. In 25 years of PeopleTek coaching, I've found among the traits that individuals like best about their leaders are honesty, integrity, the ability to listen, and authenticity. Howard displays all of these traits and so much more. If you can trust your leader because they are upfront and honest, then it gives you permission to be upfront and honest as well. I think this is a wonderful testament to Howard and his team. When I interview teams to ask about a leader's effectiveness, the qualities most cited about their best leaders are that "they were good listeners" and "cared about me as a person." Howard demonstrates great listening skills and is a role model for asking questions and really caring about his guests', callers', and staff's replies.

In 2020, *City Journal*'s Bruce Bawer wrote the article, "What Happened to Howard Stern? Once an irreverent voice of the common man and a proud outsider, the longtime shock jock has become an obsequious insider." In this piece, Bawer says Howard may be losing his popularity:

> For years, Stern's critics insisted that fans would soon grow tired of his schtick. Instead, his popularity kept soaring. His show was simultaneously #1 in New York and L.A. His two autobiographical books, *Private Parts* (1993) and *Miss America* (1995), were #1 best-sellers (and his book signings drew massive crowds); his autobiographical film, also entitled *Private Parts* (1997), opened at #1. Quivers, Martling, Lange, and Dell'Abate wrote best-selling memoirs, too. Yet though he became internationally known, Stern remained, above all, a New York fixture. The poster for his movie *Private Parts* featured a picture of a naked Stern with the Empire State Building covering his naughty bits. Long before *The Apprentice* made Donald Trump famous outside New York, he was a regular guest on Howard's show—and a genuine friend. (Stern attended Trump's wedding to his second wife, and Trump attended Stern's wedding to *his* second wife.)
>
> Trump and Stern bonded over two things: their love of beautiful women and their commonsensical world views. For even as he lampooned

religious conservatives and organized religion generally (gags about the pope and Cardinal O'Connor were a show staple), Stern had no illusions about the Left. He stood up for hardworking family men; he believed in law and order; he respected the police and military; and he called out David Dinkins's disastrous mayoralty as lustily as he later cheered Rudy Giuliani's reforms. (In 1994, Stern won the Libertarian Party nod for governor of New York—among his top issues was getting highway repairs done at night—but he withdrew from the race rather than comply with financial disclosure requirements.)

And for *The New York Times*, in 2019, David Marchese wrote "Howard Stern says he has changed. How much?" From the way he's portrayed, it seems that Howard acknowledges a paradigm shift in his career.

> Howard Stern will forever loom large in radio history as the medium's bawdiest personality, a man whose hugely popular shock-jock antics during the 1980s and '90s spawned a legion of drive-time loudmouths. Since moving from terrestrial to satellite radio in 2005, though, he has altered his legacy in ways that only an especially optimistic oracle might have foreseen. Stern, 65, has gradually become a master interviewer, one consistently able to elicit honest emotion and genuine insight from his celebrity guests. His first new book in more than 20 years, *Howard Stern Comes Again*, showcases this transformation

and his refined conversational style. "I had interviewed every porn star about every orifice," Stern says of his wilder days. "Don't get me wrong, I was fascinated, but I couldn't be that guy anymore."

To his fan base, Howard is dearly loved and honored as brilliant, innovative, creative, idolized, a fabulous interviewer, and a visionary. Everyone else might be surprised by how his new book, interviewing style, and behavior hold up the controversial figure as an example of leadership. How is that possible?

I could have selected other leaders to profile. In fact every leader on the planet has strengths and areas to develop — be it Donald Trump or any other notable figure. Yes, even Donald uses some of the process as I see it — although, he chooses not to pay attention to other parts of it. I selected Howard because I wanted someone who was accountable and was a Continual Leadership Learner — those qualities were musts. This means you are never a master at this process. You can be very good in many areas, but you must be able to learn, grow, and transform your life and the lives of others by what you do. Howard has done this and is a Continual Leadership Learner, as recently proved by his total change in approach to interviewing — reducing his sarcasm when interviewing and really getting to know the person on a deeper level. He now really cares.

Why is this book important? It is for you. Your career. Your future. By following along with the steps outlined here, you can ensure your leadership skills improve and your career moves forward, and you'll feel more aligned and confident because you have the tools and a process to apply throughout your career. If you read and attempt the techniques outlined, your leadership will improve. Howard's examples will give you some ideas about what to try in practice at your office. What we will do together in this book is provide a learning process for leadership. All of us are leaders. We will use the Leadership COMPASS, which has twelve learning areas. Each area will be described in detail. Then I will present an example of each area using Howard's behavior or show to demonstrate or bring clarity to that learning area.

The best way to use this book will be to rate your own behavior and then see how you can learn, grow, and transform in each of the twelve areas as you move through the book. Remember, leadership development is a *process* — not an *event*. This means that even if you make progress, you will need to keep building your leadership muscles.

So, without further ado, let's get to work!

Introduction: Personal Accountability

I've been listening to Howard for over 25 years, and I can think of no one who displays real leadership in action for himself, his team, or SiriusXM more than Howard.

I wanted to write about someone who practiced Continual Leadership Learning. As PeopleTek CEO for over 30 years and leading 40-plus coaches guiding many customers, I've worked with leaders, teams, and organizations and have witnessed that what comes so easily to Howard is very difficult for others. Howard's behavior on his show provides the action all of us need to witness in order to free ourselves and become the leaders we are destined to be. His ability to speak the truth as he sees it, argue, push, pull, direct, give in — all of it teaches us that we are leaders, both in our good and bad behavior.

You need to look at yourself in the mirror and determine how you can apply these tools and leadership methods. Before working on myself, I would blame others for my faults as a leader. Not that I did anything terrible, but I thought if my boss did this or the company did that or our customers did other things, then everything would be better. This was totally not the case. Until I took ownership of and accountability for my actions and Leadership Learning, nothing was going to improve. I love how a great personal friend, who is also a client and one of the most creative business innovators I know, Steven Pruett, put it: "We must let go of our ego, develop others, and bring them along the way with us." Steven has been doing this now for years, and I've seen it pay off over and over again with the individuals he leads and companies he's grown.

PeopleTek's definition of leadership is to empower yourself and others to go where you've never gone before. Howard fits this idea perfectly. He has empowered himself to lead others in order to make this world a more joyous experience. He has linked his what we call "Magic Dust" (skills, abilities, and talents that are unique to him) with his life's daily work. Some would say he exploits women, exploits their bodies, and is vulgar. I say those who believe this are not listening and have personal shame that puts a barrier around their own joy and happiness. The sad thing is many of those individuals are leading others in business. They can be barriers to joy and happiness in themselves and in the workplace. I would ask many people, "Have you ever heard of Howard?" They would likely answer no.

Consider PeopleTek's quote, "Without conflict, there is no leadership." There is no one I know in the public eye who brings conflict to the center of attention as much as Howard. He does this every day. Howard does this every day on his show with so many discussions of controversial topics. Yes, some are obnoxious and immature, but they are no less controversial.

Howard is not afraid to take on any of his staff, his audience, and guests, and he does it in a healthy, honoring, and respectful manner. How do I know? Because I hear it on the air. He empowers us all to do better with our lives, the way we eat, exercise, and take care of ourselves. He points out issues that are absurd and brings them to our attention. He may use a very extreme person or situation, such as one of his team members being late all the time (Benjy), and discuss this behavior with his entire audience.

This is exactly what a healthy team can do. They can bring up behavior with each other and discuss it without fear or behind someone's back. Yes, there is sarcasm, and the show could be better if that weren't part of it; however, being upfront but sarcastic is better than talking behind someone's back. Everything Howard has said about people he likes or doesn't like is made public on the show. Some would say he should hold back and not say anything. I look at it as him being confident in what he says and being willing to discuss it with anyone. I have heard him back down when presented with feedback that he went too far. An example of this came when he was recently with the LIV Golf tour in the United States, which was sponsored by Saudi Arabia. He said that, after criticizing some of the golfers, a listener called him out in a nice way, and he said, "You know what, maybe I don't know the entire story."

There are so many examples of his using healthy conflict to get us moving forward. For example, going back years, when he wanted to run for governor of New York, he had a platform to eliminate all tolls. While this may seem like a small matter, it needed to be discussed, and I for one agree with Howard: it is still ridiculous to keep people waiting in line to pay tolls. Further examples can be found in his discussions with his team and their peculiar personalities: Benjy being late, Ralph being obsessed, Fred being introverted, Robin's relationships, the entire Wack Pack. All of his guests have very interesting backgrounds that he brings up, and some may view this as conflict. But he is not afraid of it and in fact embraces it.

If we as leaders don't bring up things that are important — such as our behaviors that are not working and processes that need adjusting — then we are not being leaders. Whose responsibility is it to bring these things up? All of ours. We are all leaders and own everything happening around us. We must make a decision, open up, say things in a healthy manner, and determine as a team how to move forward.

The problem is that many of us hold back, don't say anything, talk behind our team's backs, and worse yet talk to others who have nothing to do with the concern. Some of us are afraid of what others may think of us, how they will react, or what will happen, so we do nothing. Howard, while exaggerating situations, models how we should practice bringing up important issues that bother us and are impacting our customers and other team members.

Every day Howard empowers his team — most members unwillingly — to share their lives. This is so important for everyone to hear because we all have lives that need to be examined. Maybe not in public, but we need to be the examiners of our thoughts, beliefs, feelings, and behaviors. Howard allows everyone's humanity to be exposed, and he is willing to open up his humanity. This is being vulnerable. It gives us all permission to do the same.

You might say there is no comparison between corporate America and Howard's show. While I can understand your concern, I would say the elements of leadership and creating the culture he uses are the same. He builds a trusting, honoring, empowering environment where every individual can excel. In the corporate world, business people would love to have the trust that Howard has created with his team — and the loyalty. Very few people ever leave the show — Jackie the Joke Man and a few others are the only ones I know of after decades.

Most important are Howard's interviews. His art as a leader is to get others to open up. He becomes vulnerable, and this permits his guests to do the same. We all become better leaders by listening because we get to hear how others have empowered themselves, gotten through adversity in their lives, and become famous for being outstanding in their craft. Whether discussing music, drama, comedy, or life overall, Howard knows how to bring out the best in everyone.

I will use examples from these interviews to show how we also can be great leaders of ourselves — that is where everything starts.

This book will show us examples of Howard's leadership approach and how he uses the processes from the Leadership COMPASS every day. I use Howard's interviews to provide examples for you on how to become better at leading yourself and others. The vulnerability he accomplishes gives all of us the permission to be leaders, have issues and problems, and share how we overcome them. Hearing these stories is so very powerful because the interviewees are no different from any person on the planet. However, they are people who found out what they were good at, lived their special gift, and went through many things to find success. No matter your age, you can be a continual learner and learn from others. These stories will provide insights for all of us.

In addition, Howard and his team on the show have helped so many. Each member of his team has helped this world be a better place. They've made a career decision to help others be happy and receive joy through sharing their lives, personalities, and choices with others. I've never read a formal vision statement for Howard's show; however, after listening, you can feel the passion, energy, and values Howard and the entire team share. What could be better than ongoing behavior for communicating a vision?

I wanted to write something fun where I can disclose my own vulnerabilities and Leadership Learning as we move along. I also wanted a venue that I don't normally use to reach everyone. I'm sure Howard's audience can benefit from my concepts like everyone else. I can also share over 30 years of experience consulting and coaching leaders, teams, and organizations.

Howard has made me so happy in my life — as he has for so many others. While I don't listen as much as I used to, I can't think of any better way to repay him for all of the good times and leadership and life qualities he's shared openly with the world. Thank you, Howard, Robin, Fred, Gary, Benjy, Sal, Ronnie, Ralph … and the entire team, including numerous colleagues and guests of the show, of which there are too many to mention.

Back to the primary topic of personal accountability. We all own our careers, our lives, and the leadership skills we develop or don't develop. I've argued with many who believe that leaders are born, and you can't develop the skills to be an effective, impactful leader. I say that is totally not true. In fact, after observing leadership skills and developing them in others for over 25 years, I've seen many individuals learn, grow, and transform their leadership skills. They have a major impact on their teams and their organizations. It is up to us as individuals to improve ourselves as leaders and empower ourselves and each other to move beyond where we are and influence in a more impactful manner.

We own everything that is happening to us. We can say it's our boss, our parents, our clients … but in the end, it is how we respond to whatever is happening to us. Are there bad breaks? For sure. How do we show up when these things happen? Do we ask the questions John Miller, the great author of the book

QBQ!, asks, "What can I do, and how can I do it?" Do we avoid asking who's to blame, and why is this happening to me? When we change the question to ask what we can do to help ourselves and others, then we are exercising personal accountability to make the situation better.

WHY HOWARD?

Howard's interviews on a daily basis are proof that he empowers us all to go where we've never gone before. He has also empowered himself. When he left the broadcast stations to go to SiriusXM satellite radio, this was a major change. He demonstrated with courage that he was empowered to make a change. Was this hard? Yes. Why? Because he was very popular on regular FM radio. Now he was going to another medium that was not tried and tested. He made a decision because he saw a future there. (Yes, he did get paid big bucks to go as well). It was still a great risk.

I can select any interview of a famous star, or just a caller, to illustrate how Howard brings out the person's essence.

In his book *Howard Stern Comes Again*, you can read the interviews he selected and see how each person shares their vision, purpose, struggles, happiness, sadness, and life. In addition, on the SiriusXM website, you can find many years of past interviews from shows that will demonstrate how Howard makes leadership come alive. I am hoping these interviews will provide you with a process and the confidence to know that you too can bring leadership to a new level.

Howard is able to bring the essence out of each person he speaks to. As leaders, we need to do the same. We need to not be afraid to dig deeper into ourselves and others. This is where our leadership lies. This is where people are struggling. Many will say that is not a leader's job. I say yes it is, and the most powerful and best can do it. Maybe not as well as Howard does on his show, but they can dig deeper so ultimately individuals learn more, grow, and become successful. Howard is open and skilled in asking crucial questions. We need to be as well. Too often as leaders we make assumptions about surface-level responses. This keeps our conversations about work and crucial processes shallow. We need to dig deeper. Pay attention to some of the examples and how Howard seeks to understand more. Yes, sometimes it's uncomfortable to get to the root of life and learning. But by doing this, Howard helps himself and everyone learn, grow, and transform.

Through the leadership lessons of Howard Stern, you will get the tools and the process to set yourself free. For example, the process for Vision, Mission, Goals, Measures = Behavior can give you a lifetime of prosperity if you use it and live it. By creating and implementing this for yourself, you will lead yourself and others more effectively and with greater impact. You will take courageous steps to be the leader you were always meant to be. Or at least you will begin a process to get there. You will be a true leader of leaders. Who better than Howard to show us all the way, in a fun and creative manner? He is a true inspiration for our careers and life. Hopefully I explain his method well — and if I don't, I am sure Howard and his team will give me feedback!

If you as a leader are not listening to your team members, your customers, and your vendor partners, then you are not asking the right questions. Can we go as deep as Howard? Probably not without a lawsuit. However, can we go deeper into our interactions and get to know the people we are dealing with better? Yes, we can. We can learn where they grew up, whether they relocated, what difficulties they've faced in their life, how many brothers and sisters they have, what kinds of jobs they've had and what made them difficult. If you have team members and don't know these details, it's time you learned more about them.

HOMEWORK

Interview at least two members of your team. What did you learn? How can this information help you as their leader?

1
A Better Leader Now (Where Howard and PeopleTek's Leadership COMPASS Meet)

WE ARE ALL LEADERS. Every one of us no matter our role or title is a leader. We are either positively or negatively leading, but one thing is for sure: we are leading ourselves and others. The point is that we can have much more impact when we understand no one needs to tell us we are leaders. We need to tell ourselves. We decide, just like my father did, that we are a leader (more on this in my dedication to him at the beginning of the book).

You don't need a title, and you don't need permission to be a leader, and you don't need to wait to be told you are a leader.

You are special by virtue of being alive today, and the gifts you bring to others are crucial. Howard may poke fun at guests and callers on his show; however, he also puts a spotlight on our uniqueness by making us laugh and think.

From a young age, and especially when you get your first job, you are responsible for leading yourself and others. Too often, we are not prepared with the tools or methods to be an effective leader. At many companies, there is little training on leadership, and if there is any, it's not enough, especially to make a transition from a role as a doer to managing a group of others.

If you listen to Howard's program — or if you don't listen or never plan to listen — you are a leader. I want everyone to understand they are leaders right now. Most of us really don't think so, or we've been told that we are not leaders because of our title, our wealth, our position or status, and we learn to minimize ourselves. We make ourselves small. I was recently told by a client, "I finally realized that he [my boss] wasn't my parent, and I don't need to ask him permission to speak to someone."

This book provides a process for leadership. Whether you're leading a team, your organization, or just yourself, there is a process to leadership. The process needs to be practiced and developed. It's just like anything else that is worthwhile — you must practice the process and the elements in it to get stronger in each of the leadership areas.

If you've picked up this book, you probably want to be a better leader. But you may even think you are not a leader.

The purpose of this book is to help you immediately change that thought to I AM A LEADER NOW. Now, I am going to be a great leader.

You've taken step one and begun a process to develop as a leader. We have limited time in our lives and limited roles to play in our careers. We may as well do things on purpose and not by mistake. By using the tools and process in this book, you will be taking courageous steps to be the best leader you can be. By following the direction of the Leadership COMPASS and changing your mindset, you will take charge of your career. You will be free of saying everyone else has control of my life and career, and you will feel better and more confident in the business roles you play every day.

We all have many options open to us. Many of us feel we know what direction to take, but then we may ask ourselves whether we took the right direction, and we may wonder what caused us to make certain choices during our leadership careers. Most of us have to learn, on the fly, on our own. Or we learned from a current boss, a past boss, or simply picked things up along the way.

There is a better approach. For years, effective leaders have been taught how to be the best they can to deliver high-performance teams and organizations. Let's change the past and learn how to be effective and impactful from the start. Why not have something that can guide us to stay out of the storm? The COMPASS will provide a process and framework to follow.

It will enable us to make more informed and well-thought-out decisions about our own leadership.

This book is for you. It is not for Howard, Howard's team, or me. You are special. If you've picked up this book, you are a leader. This is probably the most important concept to understand about leadership. We do not need a title. We do not need a role. We are leaders every single day. All of us.

Please just pretend that I am right. I am telling you this, and you now believe it. I am encouraging you: if you have this mindset and read further in this book, you will learn tools, develop skills, and make changes you never thought possible.

How do I know this? You've already empowered others to go where they've never gone before. That is one part of our definition of leadership. You can't just work on yourself; you must work with and help others on their path too. So the definition we will live by is "leadership is empowering yourself and others to go where you haven't gone before." So starting today, and from this moment forward, you must consider yourself on a path to be a leader. Reading this book will give you tools, tips, and techniques to apply daily that will help you with this objective.

The first of those tools is the Leadership COMPASS.

There are twelve points of focus in this Leadership COMPASS. The remainder of the book will define each of the focus areas and then have you apply an evaluation to each area. There will be assignments for every focus area that will increase your effectiveness and impact as a leader.

The Leadership COMPASS areas of action can be found in the opening section of this book. You can also find them on our website at *www.peopletekcoaching.com*

Why the need for a COMPASS? I believe that leadership development is a process and not an event. For many years, leaders have been thinking they are fully developed after attending one or two courses or reading a book. Leadership skills and the ability to be good at them take time to develop. How we develop ourselves and coach others to be successful is crucial and a lifelong process of learning. I believe that a leader never ends their improvements.

Just like going to a gym, it is crucial to keep building our leadership muscles. Once we know our strengths, it is important to use them and to help others use their strengths. Once our awareness grows and we uncover our blind spots, it is important we surround ourselves with team members who can support our blind spots through the use of their own strengths.

When our vision, mission, goals, and measures are established, it is crucial to keep leading others and gaining alignment to execute the organization's objectives.

Who needs a Journey and a COMPASS? I've already pointed out that every person is a leader. I assume you are good at doing a job or a task. Have you been promoted? Why? Why not? The COMPASS is an interpersonal road map of how you show up and what will be required for you to now succeed as a leader. Everyone in any position needs a Journey if they deal with people or handle conflict, or if they are part of a team, a project, or a group of any kind and they have to not only get along with others but be the most effective team member they can be.

When is the best time to use your COMPASS? Now. For many years, customers have said to me, "When is the best time to take your programs like The Leadership Journey and begin to use the COMPASS?" The best time is right now! Usually after they start to use the COMPASS or graduate from The Leadership Journey, the graduates ask "Why didn't I take this sooner?" That is why the best time to start is NOW.

Since our definition of true leadership is to empower ourselves and others to go where they've never gone before, everything must start with you. For too many years I relied on others but not myself. I wanted their permission to do things. I saw many clients and team members doing the same thing. I am telling you now that if you only change this aspect of your approach, miracles will happen. Don't wait for anyone to give you permission. You are a leader now. Take advantage of it.

You must empower yourself first. So you need to decide, What is your motivation? What do you want to make better? The COMPASS will take you there, but you need to know what you want to accomplish and why.

For many years I was just doing things because I wanted to make money, or impress myself, my family, and my friends, or because I wanted not to feel fear. These reasons are all okay, and I know for sure many of you may be taking a job, role, or assignment for the same reasons. I took jobs working in a bowling alley, a department store, and with computers, as the skills for this work kind of just came to me. This is what is so cool: all of your work will play a role in what you really wish to do and the reason you wish to do it. Why? Because you take yourself everywhere, and I know that I — and most of us — don't fully value ourselves the way we could.

Even Howard says no matter how much fame he had in his career, he wasn't happy or satisfied with himself, and he still feels bad about himself and "less than." Can you imagine that someone with all that talent and fame still feels that way? I am the same. I've gotten much better by using the processes outlined in this book. It doesn't mean I don't have to keep learning or developing my skills in the areas I know need improvement. The good news is I have the tools, support from coaches, and other means of improvement that I will continue to use on a daily basis. I have a dream to attain individual, team, and organizational excellence, and Howard is the role model for us all to follow.

For example, Howard's show empowers us to be bold. He was bold. He has talked, and still talks, about things that no one would have brought up in the past. He openly shares and gets others to do the same. Prior to Howard, there was no one really doing this. He set the framework of this type of talk radio into motion. He empowered himself to go beyond anything thought possible previously. This gives us the permission to do the same.

He recently was discussing his first radio job after he graduated. After two weeks, the general manager of the station fired him. He could have called it quits forever, and he said that many would have. But Howard didn't do that. He empowered himself to go through the pain and fear. This is what is meant by empowering yourself to go where you've not previously gone before.

Howard also built a team, empowering others. In the industry he is in, I haven't seen it where other radio show experts build a team around themselves. Other radio personalities usually have one or two other people who assist them, not an entire team. Howard has many such people. This is impressive as the show has aired for so many years and very few from the team leave.

The Leadership COMPASS is a tool you will use while reading this book. It is a visual representation of twelve important areas of leadership. All parts of the COMPASS are very important, but the most important is Continual Leadership Learning. This makes you personally accountable to be better. If you don't practice this, you may be called a good leader; however, I would challenge that, because your lack of continual learning [or Continual Leadership Learning] [or willingness to learn continually] shows arrogance. We are arrogant when we think we can't get even better within ourselves, and with others, our companies, and our society. There is so much to learn, and to think we have learned it all and can't improve is not good for any leader.

What we need to become aware of is how to be the best leader. The first step to take on this journey is to develop the awareness that YOU ARE A LEADER NOW. Like a real compass, there are points on the outside that show us the direction we are headed. This leadership tool is the same but points to the direction of leadership we are headed toward and working on. We will measure where we are in each step and then make a decision on how we wish to proceed. This will be a process that empowers us to learn each of the twelve areas below, make some plans, and then start to implement those plans. You can say, "I am working on my career to ensure I am the best leader I can be by implementing actions each day that make me better."

Here is an example of a client who used the COMPASS to be a better leader. At first she didn't see herself correctly. Why? Because she was blind to how her strengths were being overused. Annie, a colleague of mine, after attending one of our courses said she thought she was open and assertive; however, when her sister pointed out Annie wasn't listening, she realized she had a habit of resisting information from others. That is why it's important not only to rate yourself but also to begin a candid conversation with others about the COMPASS and get their impressions.

Once Annie had this realization, she was able to improve her listening skills.

You must lead yourself before you can effectively lead anyone else. It is all about your awareness as a leader; then it becomes about the awareness of others. Too often leaders are promoted into positions without the proper skills and awareness to lead others. They are waiting for others to tell them what to do and when.

When I first started working at a large financial institution, I was a terrible boss for others when I was first promoted. I didn't listen, talked over others, was unfair, and had no vision for where I was going. My superiors said that I was a visionary who motivated others, inspired them, and had great relationships. They also said I was wishy-washy and didn't hold others accountable. Wow, this was not fun to hear.

Many are like me, good at doing a job or task as engineers, sales professionals, accountants, lawyers, nurses, doctors, programmers — the list goes on and on. Then we get promoted into leadership positions because we did so well in those basic roles. That is when our trouble begins.

WHY HOWARD?

As I promised, we will use Howard along the way to show us. I will take Howard interviews, show dynamics, and personality traits and connect them to the COMPASS as examples of application.

I recently tuned in to a Howard interview where Joe Namath was sharing his past, his struggles, and his current life. Joe shared how he is an alcoholic and has struggled with this for most of his life. This truly is leadership. Not only did Joe become vulnerable and show his humanness, but he also shared why it was crucial for him to change. This gives others permission to change. By Howard asking the right questions and providing the opportunity for Joe to share, Howard and Joe may have improved the lives of others. By empowering just one other person, they made this a better planet. This is leadership because we don't know which others will be impacted and how they in turn will influence other leaders.

Howard does push the envelope with everything. This leadership technique for the purpose of this book is perfect because it brings the things we should be discussing out into the open and lets us be human and "real" about them. These topics include bathroom techniques, sexuality, relationships and friendships, gift giving, business, entertainment, love, death, politics, news ... everything. By being vulnerable with his audience, Howard builds trust.

This is something everyone must do — build trust. A team immediately can sense when we are not authentic. It's fine to be a stuffed shirt if you are one. Don't be ashamed of it. At the same time, it's fine to be funny, loose, and free-flowing like Howard. When listening to his show, you immediately pick up that he is real. Let's face it — Howard leads his staff and audience to be more empowered to advance themselves beyond where they are now.

You may say I am crazy. Why does talking about taking a poop in a certain way matter? Or for that matter, masturbation techniques and frequency, and so many other topics too numerous to mention?

By Howard discussing these everyday human events live on the radio, he gives us, the audience, permission to do the same, to be more authentic and to discuss anything that is impacting our lives. Howard gives us permission to laugh at ourselves and live a little bit of joy.

I just heard a recording of someone who said we are all here to suffer. Well, I want to be suffering and listening to Howard Stern. Why? Because, even in my suffering, I am laughing out loud. This is the legacy of true leadership, and if we all listened and learned rather than criticizing him, we would all be better people for it.

If you match his skills to PeopleTek's Leadership Journey and COMPASS, he 100 percent uses all of the aspects to cater to his listeners and uses his organization to deliver the highest quality product and service possible. Well, maybe one exception is that we teach that everyone should provide feedback in a healthy, honoring, respectful manner.

Sometimes on the show they try to be respectful but then it gets — let's just say — out of hand. However, I still believe they work at it, with everyone participating and working to get the other person to see and understand their behavior. Sometimes, even with everyone working at it, they have to just SCREAM and let it go.

If I personally take a look at my behavior, I have to admit that I admire Howard's skill at living a dream and implementing it without fear of what others would say. I want this book to be my reality. What I mean by this is that I want to tell everyone exactly how I feel about everything as it relates to myself and where I have hidden my true self. I think Howard shows himself every day to millions of people, and they love him for it. I want to finally do the same.

For too long I tried to please everyone — my parents, my friends, my bosses, my team, my children. I love them all, but I gave them too much power. I have this high need to be loved and liked by everyone, and it has been a curse to my leadership legacy.

I think that comparing leadership to Howard provides me an avenue to be the authentic Mike Kublin. I just need to be authentic, and hopefully, by helping myself I will finally help many others.

Although I am extremely grateful for all I've gotten to do and been involved with in my career, I think I may not have been as ready to live my dream as Howard has. Those who know me may laugh at this, but I can tell you that Howard's creativity shines each and every day. While I know that mine does as well, it is not the same. I would love to not be so afraid to live the dream of total fun, not caring who needs to be pleased or wondering whether I will be judged as a "bad" person if I demonstrate total freedom of expression. If I said what I truly felt about life, living, or sexuality, would people leave me? I know intellectually they wouldn't; however, emotionally I am a prisoner of my upbringing and my need to please everyone and not hurt anyone.

This is not Howard. He lives his dream and is not afraid to share with others. He has first to lead himself and then offers the possibility to others to do the same. When Howard was on traditional radio, he was restricted and couldn't say or do things that some would judge as not socially acceptable.

I think over the years, I've learned from my son and others who just live that the issue I mentioned keeps society locked in place; we're like robots, with minimal to no growth. This means there is absolutely no way to lead because, when it comes to what is acceptable, we are all programmed and controlled by our past and society.

If you listen to Howard, what you will learn is how to live. He empowers you to go where you would not normally take yourself. He has changed society in a positive way and made it fun at the same time. Let's all empower ourselves to be real with each other. To share our fears and insecurities, and to live our dreams in a healthy, honoring, and respectful manner. We will have more fun, and we will live a happier and more productive life. What better way to lead ourselves and others. I want examples of Howard's demonstrated leadership concepts such as understanding self-awareness, awareness of others, communication, conflict, and relationships to help individuals across the planet build their confidence and be better leaders.

I need for each of you to start a journal. This journal will be a document that you carry with you throughout your time reading this book. You will be recording activities and thoughts about yourself and your leadership.

HOMEWORK

I need each of you to rate where you stand in each area of this COMPASS. Please rate yourself from 1 to 5 in each area. A rating of 5 means you're doing it, and you're all set. A rating of 1 means that area needs work. Please list the scores in a journal for later review. Before we go any further, please rate yourself in each of these areas. If you don't understand an area, please skip it and go to the next one. We will address and clarify all focus areas as we go through the book and process.

By now you've rated yourself from 1 to 5 in each area, and you've skipped those areas you didn't understand. I hope you are not beating yourself up for not having all 5s or for having skipped many areas. That is the entire point. Now you can empower yourself to go beyond where your leadership is. You've given yourself permission to learn, grow, and transform your skills. I've seen leaders make vast changes by just deciding to rate themselves; and then they realize the need to change one thing for themselves. I have seen others do nothing, and they stay the same over many years. Pat yourself on the back. You gave yourself a new opportunity.

With your COMPASS scores in hand, we are ready to begin.

Find or obtain a journal to keep track of each section in this book which will relate to the Leadership COMPASS and your personal leadership.

We all have the ability wired in us to influence others. We make a choice to do it positively or negatively. Most of the time, we probably don't realize it. We usually give our power to others and not ourselves. We also may not realize how influential or powerful we are. Most of us go through our lives not realizing all the tremendous power we have and minimizing our impact and relevance. We may not have all the tools we need or are not aware of the tools we already have. This book will bring to light all the skills, abilities, and talents we have within ourselves. It should, if followed closely and daily, empower you to go where you've not gone before. The book will give you permission to live your true vision, mission, and goals — and not what someone else thinks. The intention of this book is to lead you. Much like Howard does in his show. Yes, some things are nonsense, but most are included intentionally to get you to laugh out loud at yourself and others in order to learn. For example, when Howard pokes fun at himself regarding his cleanliness issues. Yes, I am sure psychologists could easily find this in their diagnostic manuals; however, it is a reality for so many people out in the world. Howard gives us all permission to talk about these things out in the open. He points reality out to us as a mirror. He does this daily with team members, the audience, his guests, and others. Why is that good leadership? Because he becomes vulnerable, human, real, a person. These qualities are what's lacking in leadership today. Everyone is afraid to say what is really going on. People are afraid of not being accepted. People are afraid of being fired. They are afraid of what others will think. They give up their power and minimize their true potential. No more. This stops right now with this book. But you must take the first step and start reading.

Using a process, we will point out where each of us stand and how we can get better at being impactful leaders. It's like going to a gym. We are all different sizes and shapes, and we have different strengths and weaknesses; however, we can all get in better shape. We must work on it daily. It is not a matter of reading and then putting the book away. My desire is for you to use the book and the lessons here to empower yourself to be the leader you were always meant to be.

The book will provide each person with a road map for their success. If you use the summary points and questions in every section, you will become a better leader. The first step is to say yes, I am going to read this book, answer the questions about myself, and then empower myself to be a better leader of myself and others. Then start by applying the suggestions made by each area of the COMPASS tools and actions. For example, start a process for self-reflection. Use some tools such as Myers-Briggs, the DiSC, Effective Listening, TKI (Thomas Kilmann Instrument), and so many more. Consider getting a psychologist or coach or mentor, completing a 360-degree assessment, or using any of so many other options to look at your behavior and how you are either serving yourself in a good way or not.

Howard speaks to everyone. His team, interviews, past, present, personality — all will be used as examples of the impacts we have and how we can be more aware of the choices and tools we use to be most effective.

If you have an official title, that's fantastic — you will now have the tools to be better at what you do. If you've been in a leadership position forever, you will have a process to follow where you may have been guessing before. One of my current clients, who is a successful VP, said to me, "Mike, the tools and process you shared not only improved my work leadership and position, they've helped me with my wife at home."

Please stop here. Don't go further without saying out loud: I am a leader NOW. I already have the ability to lead myself and others. I've already been doing it, and now I will be even better.

Is Howard perfect? Like all of us, he has strengths and weaknesses. His weaknesses, like ours, come from an overuse of our strengths. In this book, we call our strengths Magic Dust. When we overuse it, our dust becomes our weakness. We will work on this weakness a lot. You must be able to identify your strengths and then discuss what happens when you overuse them. During your journey through this book, you will gain insights into your strengths and then determine how an overuse could impact yourself, your team, and your organization.

2
The Importance of Self-Awareness and CourageAbility

When we look at self-reflection, I use the Johari Window (more on this shortly) to demonstrate what we will reveal about ourselves, what we will hide from others, what we are blind to that others can see, and what is totally unknown.

Where does it all start for each of us? Our past. I want everyone to know their past is part of what makes them a leader. No, it doesn't matter if your past was good, bad, troubled, or anything else. We are all leaders. The key is to recognize this fact and begin from where you are.

We need to ask ourselves questions like these:

What's missing from your life and your career?

- How has your past influenced this?
- Do you regret any past decisions that you've made? If yes, what have you learned from them?
- What makes you happy?
- What could you change to help you achieve that goal?

What are the obstacles that are getting in the way?

- Have any past decisions helped you move closer to your goal? How and why?
- What makes you anxious?
- What makes you relax and feel content and comfortable?
- What inspires you to do more and expand your comfort zone?
- What makes you feel valued?
- What's needed to grow your career?

Our past helps us understand our link to the ways we lead now. Everyone's past is important, even if it doesn't seem positive. Our past helps us understand how we lead now, but we have the power to change our habits at any time. In your journal, please answer the following questions about yourself. Take your time. Be open and honest in your answers. Don't worry if you think you didn't answer with enough detail. Things will begin to unfold as you read further.

This disclosure/feedback model of awareness known as the Johari Window was named by merging the first names of its creators, Joseph Luft and Harry Ingham. It was first used in an information session at the Western Training Laboratory in Group Development in 1955.

As you can see in the following illustration, there are four main components of the Johari Window for us to explore. First, there is the Open Self. In the Open Self, you have information about yourself that is known to you and to others.

Our job as leaders is to increase the Open Self and make it larger. Why? When we do this, we are confident about who we are, what we stand for, and what information we want others to know about us. When speaking about strengths or weaknesses, this idea is crucially important. For too long, I was afraid to share what I saw at work. I was worried about things like these: Will they think I am right? Would they agree? What will they think of me? The list goes on. I found out that the insights I held, when presented properly, were exactly what was needed. As you will discover, the insights that you hold are extremely important. I hear many graduates of our program say that they were afraid to speak up and be themselves. Being one's authentic self is exactly what companies look to hire. When our gift is used properly and not overused, this is what organizations need and are really paying for.

The box right below the Open Self shows the Hidden Self. This box is based on how much we trust others — if we let others see portions of ourself that we may be ashamed of or don't want to be teased about, or portions we keep below the surface because we are afraid of what others may think about this part of us.

Right next to the Open Self is the Blind Self. This is information we don't know about ourselves, but others can see it. Have you ever been given feedback by anyone such as a boss, parent, teacher, coach, or best friend that kind of punched you in the stomach? It hit you hard. We don't feel good about it, but it's crucial for us to know this information.

For example, after I was leading a large IT group for a while, I got feedback saying that I was a visionary, I was motivating, and I was creative and inspiring. But the feedback also said I was wishy-washy and didn't hold others accountable. This was extremely powerful feedback that I had to have. It actually changed my life once I was made aware of it and could share it with others.

I had to figure out where it came from and why it was coming from my strengths — my strength in helping and supporting others. When I overuse this strength, it gets in my way big time.

This Unknown Quadrant is where the power of life and innovation goes. We must explore our thoughts, feelings, dreams, and aspirations — now and in the future. The Unknown Self is the study of our feelings, thoughts, behaviors, beliefs, actions, dreams, and aspirations. When we as leaders deeply study ourselves and guide others to do the same, true innovation occurs. Innovative thinking results in a bottom-line improvement for all individuals and businesses. We need to take a risk and explore these unknown areas and make them known.

See the Johari Window[2] below. The list below this illustration will give us a start.

JOHARI WINDOW

	KNOWN TO SELF	NOT KNOWN TO SELF
KNOWN TO OTHERS	OPEN	BLIND
NOT KNOWN TO OTHERS	HIDDEN	UNKNOWN

<<<<<<<<<< TRUST >>>>>>>>>>>>>

The four panes of the window represent the following:

- OPEN: The **open** area is that part of our conscious self — our attitudes, behavior, motivation, values, way of life — of which we are aware and which is **known** to others. We move within this area with freedom. We are "open books."
- HIDDEN: Our **hidden** area **cannot be known to others unless we disclose it**. There is that which we freely keep within ourselves and that which we retain out of fear.

---

[2] J. Luft, and H. Ingham (1955) "The Johari window, a graphic model of interpersonal awareness," Proceedings of the western training laboratory in group development. Los Angeles: UCLA.

The degree to which we share ourselves with others (disclosure) is the degree to which we can be known.
- BLIND: There are **things about ourselves which we do not know** but that others can see more clearly, or things we imagine to be true of ourselves for a variety of reasons but that others do not see at all. When others tell us what they see (feedback) in a supportive, responsible way — and we are willing to hear it — we are able to test the reality of who we are and are able to grow (Blind Self).
- UNKNOWN: We are richer and more complex than that which we and others know, but from time to time something happens — is felt, read, heard, dreamed — and **something from our unconscious is revealed**. Then we "know" what we have never "known" before (Unknown Self).

It is through disclosure and feedback that our Open pane is expanded and that we gain access to the potential within us, represented by the Unknown pane.

Here are some additional questions I want you to ask yourself:

- Where did you grow up?
- What was your family's structure? Was there a divorce or loss of a parent?
- Did you move?
- What were the difficult moments during your childhood?
- In school, were there any specific things brought up that caused you happiness? Anger? Pain? Write these down.
- Did you have friends?
- Were you bullied?
- Was there religion? How did you react to it?

- What did you look like? Were you overweight? Underweight?
- Did your parents have addictions? What kind (for example, sex, drugs, or alcohol)? Did you use these kinds of substances? If so, how did you stop, or are you still using them?
- How did your parents treat you?
- Did you have food, clothing, and shelter?
- What were the most challenging things you faced?
- How did you learn to get help?
- Did others help you?
- Are you goal-oriented? Do you like structure? How do you relate to people?
- How do you deal with conflict?
- How do you deal with relationships?

WHY HOWARD?

Howard is an expert at interviewing. He brings the interview subject alive, and in every interview, has them demonstrate their leadership and what made them a leader. He helps them to be comfortable and vulnerable. I recently tuned in and heard Gary in the hot seat, speaking about his mother and their relationship. Gary is the program manager of the show. His job is to ensure that Howard is pleased and we are pleased. That is how he leads. Gary was totally open about his life with his mom and how she behaved. Howard set the stage by asking great questions and providing a platform for Gary to open up about his mom. When Gary was young, he was exposed to a mom (much like I was myself) who had issues with life and handling her day-to-day behavior. She took pills — uppers, downers — and sometimes mixed them together. This kind of behavior from a parent created a lot of stress in me, and I am sure it did for Gary as he indicated on the show. This impacted Gary and set the stage for his leadership.

I can relate totally to Gary because my mom had similar life experiences with pills and behavior. This formed my personality, as it did Gary's. We ended up in the jobs we held, and we performed them the way we did, because of what had happened to us. Gary is a pleaser, and so am I. We care about others and want to please them — Gary in his role as a leader on the show. Gary is easy to tease, kid around with, and make fun of. He doesn't let anything impact how he shows up. He has a positive outlook no matter the circumstances. On the show, Gary shared that his people-pleasing creates a lot of frustration in his current marriage. It did the same for me and had a ramification of how I led others. The realization that this impacts us is also what provides our gifts of understanding, being supportive of others, and so on. In other words, for Gary and I, people-pleasing ties to our Magic Dust and how we demonstrate it. However, it also ties to when we overuse our skills. It triggers our needing to be liked and respected.

Gary gets along with others, constantly takes abuse, and shows up with a positive outlook no matter what the circumstances. He cares about others, and it shows. He leads by working with Howard and the team and helping the world of comedy through their show. This show has great meaning to Gary, and his efforts behind the scenes don't go unnoticed. The show wouldn't be nearly as good without Gary.

Fred has been with the show since the beginning. He plays all the sound effects. Fred is very quiet and introverted. Howard pretty much leaves him alone to do his thing. Fred is fascinating, and when he does come out with something to say, it usually means we need to listen as it will be insightful. Howard teased

Fred by saying he would probably be a boring interview. Yes, he would be quiet and offer few words explaining his life and beliefs. It would be so fun for the audience to hear more from Fred. Fred is a master at his craft, as is Gary in programming.

I will also give examples of Robin and her difficult past with incest and relationships. She leads in a quiet way, as a perfectionist, and everything she says has meaning and relevance. The show would not be where it is without Robin, Gary, and Fred. Howard of course is a master at letting everyone use their special leadership skills to impact the listener.

Each of us gets permission in our lives to do the same. We are leading now. Are we leading the way we want to? Are we using our skills, talents, and abilities on purpose or by mistake? Our past is so very important to how we lead now. Please take some time now to jot down your personal history. Where did you grow up? How many siblings do you have? What was a difficult thing you faced while growing up? How did your parents treat you? What good things happened? What bad things? How do these events influence your current role and behavior? Write your answers in a journal.

What I love about Howard and the show is that everything is brought into the open. This is so very important for teams — and great leaders know and understand this.

Not only does Howard open himself up to being vulnerable every day, but by doing so he gives permission to his entire team to do the same. I believe this action increases their ability to trust. I also believe his method decreases his team's blind spots, because he's making fun of their issues in a live broadcast.

An effective team can give and receive feedback with each other and laugh at it. Some take offense, and the feedback may not be given with total dignity and respect; however, it is used as a tool to improve their performance and make individuals better. The show knows that, and the group very rarely loses team members because they all know they are safe there. Howard explores the unknown. This is where true innovation lies, and he permits his team to explore their creativity. He does this by allowing them to look at their careers, and he gives coaching advice on how to approach their work. The team discusses issues in front of the entire world. The back-office operation there has issues, and these are discussed without any pretense, including exposing behavior that is off the wall. Effective teams can do this. It is Howard who sets the tone.

My career since 1988 has been devoted to helping leaders, teams, and entire organizations thrive. When I received my "wishy-washy" feedback, and it became clear that others felt I didn't hold people accountable for their behavior, I took action. I brought in a woman who specialized in working with doctors and nurses in hospitals, and she showed me how my behavior was creating these perceptions.

Here is where I think Howard has mastered leadership. He knows for a fact that he has issues. As mentioned, he openly discusses his own issues as well as those of his guests and his team on the show. He openly discusses his germaphobia, the difficulties and challenges of politics, and public perception on the show. The team laughs and makes fun. Some say this could be sarcastic; however, it's not taken that way. On the show, people learn to openly discuss these traits, issues, and concerns. This is what makes Howard's leadership so special. In addition, he has a gift I've always envied. That is the ability to let go of what others think of him.

I have a habit of not being as direct as I need to be. It can kill my leadership excellence when I hold back my desire to make and bring clarity to a point when it differs from another's point of view. If I am trying too hard to get someone to respect me, then I will not be giving my best demonstration of Leadership.

Howard and I have many similarities: creativity, caring, listening skills, trustworthiness and honesty, entrepreneurship, innovativeness, humor, family, sexuality, and the list goes on. Through the years, I've listened and laughed because I've had the same thoughts and taken the same actions. However, one major difference is that Howard is always one step ahead of me, and I believe it's because he is free and has conquered this issue of "Everyone must like me." This concern is the kiss of death for a leader because it impacts all decisions and prevents you from making crucial decisions for your life and career.

For years I've worked in therapy to help understand when and why I am doing certain behaviors that may be impacting my life and career. For example, behaviors where I try to please others rather than tell them what I am seeing. These behaviors are taking time away from being the best leader I can and helping others be their best.

Howard is either more aware or smarter than I, as he was able to succeed much faster in impacting society in a much deeper manner than I was. At least, this is my belief. I have made great progress, however. I feel all leaders must have the ability to lead, grow, and transform. This means unlimited success in all areas, including having an impact on our society in massive ways and earning money and respect.

For too long, I felt I wasn't good enough to achieve great things. I didn't deserve to. This thinking limits the mindset of growth and ultimately success. Howard is free of those constraints. He is still working on it daily and is actually expanding his reach. This is helping to build other leaders. With this book, I want to formalize this approach and expand my reach with the Leadership Journey Program. So many have grown, but why can't everyone else on the planet grow too?

One of the nice things about owning a coaching company is that we've worked with thousands of leaders at all levels. To date, I haven't met one person who doesn't have strengths but also doesn't have an Achilles' heel. The key concern is whether they are aware and open enough to explore it and admit it. Howard creates the venue and the atmosphere for his entire team to openly address this. Better yet, they actually get paid to do it and totally have fun while it's unfolding. There are so many examples of this during every show.

For example, Fred, when he speaks, is quite insightful. Howard will point out Fred's unique behavior and sometimes compare him to someone creepy and crazy. It's an exaggeration; however, it gets others to think. It's okay to be different; it's okay to be weird. Why? Because we all are. Howard honors Fred for his gift of sound and shows Fred's overuse of quiet by making fun of it. While you may get sued in business for this, I think business has gone too far the other way in pretending this weirdness doesn't exist. What a gift to others and the world.

Patrick Lencioni's book *The Five Dysfunctions of a Team* clearly points out that trust is the most crucial foundational element in building a team. Howard builds trust in each member by ensuring the awareness and sharing of behavior is open, clear, and direct. He creates the atmosphere that enables trust to be the foundation of the show. Each member has a right to share how they feel. Some feel shame during the show, but even that is made fun of. At the end of the day, the show's members know and understand that their behaviors, which could be coming from a place of shame, fear, and talent, are what make them unique and different. This is what separates them from all other nonsense shows that hide the truth about what people are thinking, feeling, and doing. It is the same poor behavior that permeates our corporate cultures and creates a cloud of mystery. Not on the *Howard Stern Show*. There is no mystery.

You can tune in almost any day or time during the show, and it will be about self-reflection. Robin has been, for years, divulging her life events. She is known to have been molested as a child. She is loyal, dedicated, brilliant, and caring. She has shown this in her dedication to Howard throughout their careers together. Robin has been very loyal to Howard, and Howard to Robin. They show an affection and admiration for each other's true gifts and abilities — for the specialness that each person brings to the other. Their behavior and mutually trusting attitude is what I am trying to convey: that each of us is very special, all having Magic Dust and a career and life vision, mission, goals, and measures. The intersection of these two concepts is where true joy occurs. Robin and Howard demonstrate the joy and passion each person can bring to their roles in business.

On any given day, you can tune in to Howard's program, and during the interview awareness is practiced. Recently I listened to a rerun of an interview with Stephen Colbert. Howard's style and approach made Stephen feel like sharing with the world. He told everyone the story of his quest to be successful as a comic while at the same time deeply suffering with depression. Howard sets the tone for leaders around the world to be open about their lives. He demonstrates to others that it is fine to share your humanness. This is not only encouraged by Howard, it is valued and honored by the show. Which is why people listen. We as an audience are now given permission to be vulnerable and human. Yes, we may get uncomfortable, but isn't life uncomfortable?

Our definition of leadership at PeopleTek is empowering others to go where they've never gone before. Here's the difference between manager, coach, and technician:

Management is planning, organizing, controlling, and following up.

Coaching is helping others to achieve their desired goals and objectives.

Technique is doing a job or a task extremely well.

While we all spend time in each of these areas, we as leaders need to move away from being the technical expert, in order to really lead, manage, and coach others.

I just happened to tune in to Howard's show and heard Chris Rock being interviewed. He spoke about his need to have Howard recommend a psychologist (and this was pre-slap!). Chris spoke about the reasons he had not contacted a therapist sooner. (Chris had feared losing his talent and edge). These fears and insecurities are the same for many, many leaders in business today. They won't expose any weaknesses or seek help because they worry they may lose an edge, be viewed as weak, or never be a good leader or recognized as one. The fact is that until we walk through our fears, we cannot help others do the same. We cannot coach or develop others. This is one of the greatest traits of a leader: to be able to grow and develop other leaders. I am so proud of Chris for sharing his story, and of Howard for providing the platform for him and so many others to do the same.

A Howard interview with Dana Carvey revealed Dana's father was very rough on him in his early years. His father's behavior did not stop him from moving his career forward. Now he is in counseling, and he is open enough to share the insight of the benefit of being open and vulnerable and getting help when you need it — from a counselor, coach, mentor. This is so powerful because it gives all of us permission to share our stories. That is what successful leaders can do. Howard set the tone, and Dana was open enough to share. And we all benefit.

Another way in which Howard is a perfect example of leadership is his ability to be courageous in his beliefs and to live them daily.

As I establish in my other book, with Jan Mayer-Rodriguez, *12 Steps for Courageous Leadership*, CourageAbility is the art and science of living your life with courage. It is living in faith rather than fear. It is living on purpose not by mistake. Too often our world is impacted by what others have told us. Some very well-intended people, including our parents, teachers, and religious leaders, tell us that if we do something that doesn't fit the norm, we will fail, be looked upon poorly, or just plain not succeed. There are numerous stories of individuals throughout history who changed the world but were told they would never be able to succeed doing it the way they wanted to. This includes Michael Jordan, Charlie Chaplin, J.K. Rowling, Thomas Edison, and so many others.

If you understand Howard's story, you will see, day after day, someone who was told to stop or was told that no one would like what he does. In his movie and his first book, he was told by many well-meaning people not to do what he does. When he went to SiriusXM Radio, this remained the same. People continued telling him that he would fail. Howard lives in faith. While he talks about his fears and he works right through them.

I want you, the reader, to look at this example and examine yourself. Are you living your dream? Or are you living your parents' dream? Someone else's dream? How do you get back on track for yourself and your life? These people were mostly well meaning, and some not so well meaning, but the point is we have only one time through this mess. We may as well do it with all our passion and energy pointing in the best direction possible for our success. In Howard's last book there is a story about Ed Sheeran, whose origin story involved sleeping on Jamie Foxx's couch. When Howard asked, "What about your plan B?" Ed said, "Anyone I know of who had a plan B never made their dream come true."

I am going to bring this concept up throughout the book. But let's address it now: are you living in faith or fear?

I am fine if you say fear. Just realize that, jot it down in your journal, and then say without question, "I will improve my CourageAbility by learning how to change my mindset toward the feeling of fear. I will begin now to be myself and the best version of myself, starting today."

HOMEWORK

Answer the questions listed at the beginning of this chapter. Each of those questions starts the process of self-reflection.

1. Please make a list of all the past roles and responsibilities you've taken on. Identify the roles you were most satisfied with. Why?

2. What role came the easiest to you? Why?

3. Ask your trusted friends, colleagues, coworkers, bosses, and others what they think comes most naturally to you. When did they see you use or apply this skill and talent?

4. How much time do you spend in each role below?

   Leader
   Manager
   Coach
   Technician

   Do you need to adjust any time spent in the role to be more effective for yourself and others?

3
Magic Dust

Magic Dust is not something you smoke. Magic Dust is the skills, abilities, strengths, and talents you bring to any job, task, or role, and that you will bring to any and all jobs in your career.

It is linked to your purpose and why you are here. It is generally displayed with ease and requires little effort. Once you realize what it is, and that you've been doing it all your life, you feel so good about yourself.

Magic Dust helps us find the roles we fit into best and how we can help teams and organizations, and it drives our passion in the work we do daily. It brings us joy to use it. It helps others. It can make us a lot of money. Once we realize how special we are as leaders, our self-confidence builds. Our focus and determination to succeed become clear. How we help and assist others is revealed. Our life work and legacy can flourish.

We can advertise our Magic Dust to others, put it on our résumés, and find work that will benefit us the most. I can tell you from experience that you will get paid for it. You will be able to keep increasing your brand recognition, and others will understand immediately what you bring to the table.

Magic Dust will help your teamwork and relationships as well. Why? Because you will now understand others and their special Magic Dust (aka the unique skills, abilities, and talents that each of us bring).

The issue with Magic Dust is it comes with a price. The price is that we have an issue when we use it too much. All of us do. We use it and don't realize we may be getting in the way of others, alienating them or, most important, not recognizing the skills, abilities, talents, and Magic Dust of others.

Your Magic Dust is crucial for you to understand. What are the skills, abilities, and talents you bring that are special? The way you do things, how you show up? Magic Dust is our passion, and we use it with ease. Without being phony or prescribed, it's the special talent you bring, no matter what role you're in. If you don't know what your Magic Dust is now, that is totally fine. This program is an investigation that should bring more clarity to your Magic Dust. I've seen people feel so much more confident once they understand their strengths. They can now explain to others these strengths and how they can benefit the teams and organizations these people work for. Magic Dust also explains to others why they may be hard to deal with. It is generally the misunderstanding of our strengths that can get in our way. We will learn in this book how to begin a process to identify our Magic Dust, reveal how it helps us, and give us insights into how it may hold us back.

You need a baseline of knowledge to understand what your Magic Dust is. You can use tools like StrengthsFinder or others to determine your special skills, abilities, talents, and the way you approach things. Tools such as Myers-Briggs, DiSC, Hogan, Enneagram, Gallup StrengthsFinder, and EQ-i 2.0 can all be found in books or for free online, or there are numerous coaches and others who use these tools and many more. The point is that the tools work. You can learn new things from each one. You have to take them and try to examine yourself through the lens of the tools.

Let's try one together. For this chapter, I want to share an exercise inspired by William Moulton Marston's[3] DiSC. Please see the lists of words and phrases at the top of the next page.

Of these words and phrases, please select the six that are most like you.

Of the six, choose the three most relevant.

Then select the one that is most like you.

If you selected a word from column 1, you are likely more dominant; if you chose from column 2, you are more inspirational; if you chose from column 3, you are more of a steady

---

[3] William Moulton Marston, *Emotions of Normal People*. (Routledge, 2013).

person; and if you chose from column 4, you tend to be more conscientious.

Exercise: Please circle the words that most apply to you. When done, tally the score for each column.

Action-oriented	Creative; provides ideas	Accommodating	Accurate
Adventurous	Energetic	Adaptable	Analytical
Bold	Enjoys change	Good listener	Conscientious
Competitive	Enjoys popularity	Calm; even-keeled	Consistent
Confident	Enthusiastic	Loyal	Controlled
Purposeful; goal-driven	Inspirational	Nurturing	Detailed
Strong-willed	Optimistic	Patient	Discerning
Takes charge	Takes risks	Thoughtful	Factual

Remember, we are all blends, so this exercise is not to pigeonhole you; it's just used to gain a perspective on ourselves and others.

> **D** is person who is very goal-oriented, desires results, pushes through obstacles
>
> **I** is a person who is enthusiastic, can be energetic, social
>
> **S** is a person who is steady, dependable, gets things done quietly
>
> **C** is a person who is analytical, fact-based, detailed

To understand our Magic Dust, we need to bring as many of these tools together as possible. We need input from others. What do they see in us? How do we operate best? Our bosses, coworkers, clients, and partners will see our Magic Dust clearly and be able to give us more information.

Please ask five friends, relatives, or business associates what strengths they can see that you have.

Tell them that you are serious and need this information. It is very important to you and your career.

What did you find out?

How can you put what you found out into one or two sentences?

Write the sentences here:_____
_____
_____
_____
_____

As you can see, if you said you are directive and goal-oriented and that results come first, all your traits and behaviors tie into your Magic Dust. If you said you care about people and are approachable and social, all these things tie in. If you say you get things done in a steady manner and don't like distractions but care greatly about quality, these tie in.

Now it is up to us to figure out our brand.

Too often, we try to be everything to everyone. We think we should be doing everything perfectly. Well, yes, we may be very good at many things, but we are outstanding at a few. Those few are what the world needs. Businesses need. Most of all *we* need. Why? Because when we are using our Magic Dust, we feel alive, and full of joy and happiness. When we are not using our Magic Dust, an assignment can feel like drudgery.

For many years, while in my first assignments, I did use my Magic Dust — building relationships, getting along well with others, and helping them solve problems. I liked what I did, but there were times I felt like a robot just trying to get promoted and please others. It was no one's fault. I had to separate myself from what was holding me back from always using my Magic Dust — and to use it for myself, and advertise it, and align my career with it.

If you don't know what your Magic Dust is, do not worry. It is a process to find out, not an event. The knowledge will come quickly if you are open to looking at yourself, your behavior, what you like, and what comes easiest for you to do. Some people have mentioned that they would even use their Magic Dust for free.

The key is you've had it all along. Magic Dust has been part of you and will remain you. For each and every person, Magic Dust is wonderful.

What happens when you do too much of what you've identified as your Magic Dust? For example, let's say based on the earlier exercise, you've identified you're an I. The words in this column tie to enthusiasm and inspiration. This is a fabulous trait, and all teams and organizations need it. They will even pay for it. But what happens when you use this too much? When you're too enthusiastic or too inspirational? What will others think?

They may tell others that you're too carefree and emotional. They may say you lack depth. They may say you are overconfident or a cheerleader. In any case, all of our gifts, or what we called Magic Dust, can be overused if we turn to them too much. This is true for everyone on the planet. In over 30 years working with leaders at all levels, I haven't met anyone yet who doesn't have special skills, abilities, and talents, and if they overuse them, they become an Achilles' heel. It gets in their way. The solution is to identify the problem and create awareness around it.

We also need to look at our motivation for using our Magic Dust. Is it used appropriately? I bring this up because let's say our Magic Dust means doing things right. If we are doing this because we don't feel good about ourselves or others when we make a mistake, this can get in our way.

A note about Magic Dust. While ours may be better for certain jobs or tasks, everyone else has Magic Dust for other roles, jobs, or tasks as well. Ours, while powerful, is very good but doesn't make us better people because we are able to do something better. What it makes us is all very special, as we all have Magic Dust. Every person on the planet. I need everyone reading this book to begin to find out what theirs is and how to describe it, to begin to advertise it and document it in your résumés. We've provided several tools to begin to find out what it is. You probably already know and are afraid of it. Your time is now to begin to get confident around it. We also need to determine what happens when we overuse ours. For example, some people who are very goal-oriented and want to get things done might overlook a person's feelings. If this is the case, we need to look at it and determine if we at times are overusing our Magic Dust.

As I've mentioned, I am people-focused, and sometimes I don't hold people accountable for things that I know need to be completed. This hurts me most of all, and my team credibility goes down.

Now that I've recognized this, I surround myself with others who are tough and can give me feedback about where I have blind spots. Others may be too hard, too fast, too aggressive. They need other people who complement their special abilities and work together to achieve common goals that tie to a unified vision, mission, and goals. We will go into this in a lot of detail. For now, let's settle on some traits that we can call our Magic Dust. This doesn't have to be finalized; just settle for now on some words that describe you and your strengths.

A LEADERSHIP STORY OF OVERUSE OF MAGIC DUST

One of my clients who graduated from the Journey had an issue with a teammate. I asked her what had happened. She said her dominance took over, and she bulldozed someone who worked for her. She said while the other woman was dominant also, it would have done no good to tell her that. What my client did was own her behavior, not what the other person did. She said the Journey gave her the tools and insights to take personal ownership and accountability into all situations that required them — and this was one. She immediately apologized, without bringing up the other person's acts of dominance. The person at first did not accept the apology, but a week later they spoke together, and all was better.

You may think. Well, how does this relate to Howard Stern? It relates in that too many of the guests fight and fight, and this is perfect for what Howard talks about. Everyone gets defensive. The issue is why not just eat it, and then talk about it in a healthy, honoring manner? We would enjoy a much better place and planet if we did this.

WHY HOWARD?

Howard is a master at being funny. His Magic Dust is the ability to interview (better than anyone), listen, and turn the moment into something funny. He is also creative and empowers us to live outside of boxes. He gets others motivated to live in a free and unrestricted manner. (You'd better, however, get vaccinated — I totally agree with him). Howard is a master at getting the interviewee to feel relaxed. He makes us open up and become vulnerable. He does this because he himself is vulnerable. He shares information about his personal life and what he likes and doesn't like. He does this all the time, and this gives us and the interviewees the same permission.

When his Magic Dust is overused, he can turn to sarcasm. Why? Because his motivation changes from being creative, insightful, and funny to being angry — and being better and smarter. It is hard to see when we are overusing our Magic Dust. We must get deeper into ourselves to understand it. Through therapy, Howard has been able to see it, feel it, and change. He doesn't change his Magic Dust. Just his motivation for using it.

Howard being so direct and challenging can come across as sarcastic and obnoxious. He himself has adjusted his approach by considering how he is asking the questions. Without speaking with Howard, I think his motivation to use it before was to win and look good or better. Now he interviews with the same kind of questions, but his approach is to dignify the person not win any award.

I think this must have happened with Robin Williams and Howard. Howard speaks about the exchange and how bad he felt after interviewing Robin. The story is in Howard's book and shows how Howard didn't behave properly. Robin felt Howard said some things that were hurtful. Howard was overusing a strength by being funny and sarcastic. Now that Howard knows he doesn't have to be cruel and sarcastic to get his points across, he is immediately free to use his Magic Dust and not be hurtful to others using theirs. I've heard Howard express remorse that he did not get a chance to apologize to Robin before he passed. This open confession gives all of us permission to admit that we can have issues and are not perfect.

Howard shares of himself masterfully, not only with his team of colleagues, but also with his guests. All of his guests get to show how they magnify greatness for the planet. Fred, Gary, Robin, Ronnie, and all the others on the team are used for their Magic Dust. Howard lets each person on the show magnify their greatness. And I mean everyone — at all levels. They are all part of the show and the team. Baba Booey, Robin, Fred, Scott, Ronnie, Ralph, Sal, Memet, and so many numerous others are able to shine and also be vulnerable. This builds trust and greatness for any organization. Why? Because team members become vulnerable and open to discuss with everyone what is going on. That is what effective teams can do. They can tell each other what is working and what is not.

It isn't always pretty. In fact, there are times when the show can get out of hand and not come together with respect and dignity. At the end of the day, however, the team knows for sure that Howard cares for them as individuals and as a team. He knows that each plays a role; and while it gets rough for the sake of comedy, he is speaking the truth about life. Our most sacred secrets are shared on international radio. What better way to learn about your team? What better way to practice feedback and communication? You have to admit, there are no secrets on this team.

Howard and the team make fun of each other's overuse of their Magic Dust. When a team member's Magic Dust is overused, they bring this information to the audience and discuss it. For example, I love it that an entire program was spent demonstrating how Fred "shows up." He is an introvert who is so creative behind the scenes. But Howard brings even Fred out. Effective leaders and teams can do this and show how it helps or hinders when Magic Dust is overused. Sorry, Fred, I picked on you, but I could do it with anyone there. Robin gets into looking at her issues, and they are brought to the forefront. She is not afraid to expose what others may consider a weakness. What it is, is humanness. This is what effective leaders can bring — not only to this show but to the world.

Howard and his team bring their humanity to the world. They show vulnerabilities that remain private and never discussed. I think his team does the planet a great service by openly discussing things that most people are ashamed of or hide. I think the world benefits from bringing them out in the open. You may say that leaders shouldn't do this, or at least, do it discreetly. I say we went too far in the way of not talking about these human challenges and characteristics of behavior. Yes, maybe we can refrain from sexuality discussions in the workplace. But certainly, without being cruel, we should be able to openly discuss our behavior, our skills, abilities, talents, and traits.

Who would have thought a show about funny, crazy things could make so many people happy? Robin is also empathic and a feeler. She senses how others will feel. She knows this and can be tough when she wants to be. It is her understanding of self that gives her such a wonderful approach. Her gift is empathy. The rest of the team sometimes teases her about it. If Robin overuses feeling, she can be taken advantage of. I think she is totally aware of this and knows when to set a boundary. I would be curious to know how she learned to do this as this would be beneficial to many of their listeners.

The thing we all need to know, and I mean everyone, is this: I haven't met a person on the planet who doesn't possess the most fabulous skills, abilities, and talents that are given to us at birth, through DNA, God, or whatever you label it. In over 30-plus years of coaching, I also have yet to meet anyone who doesn't overuse or underuse these skills.

At a recent graduation for our Leadership Journey Program, a sponsor said, "The Leadership Journey, because of Magic Dust and all the tools, is the real diversity and inclusion program." This made my heart sing. Why? Because that is what diversity is. It is the honor and respect for every person's value, for their special gift. We bring this gift to everything we do. If each of us understood what it is and learned the Magic Dust of others, we could make every job, role, and business associate special. We could hire, reward, and develop based on it. We would not have an issue because everyone on the planet has it and would be rewarded and recognized for it.

Howard does this every day in his show. He magnifies everyone's Magic Dust, including Ralph, Fred, Gary, Robin, Ronnie, Sal, and the list goes on and on.

Howard highlights the special gift in each member of his team. He does it in a fun way. He does it sometimes sarcastically, however it works. They have all profited from it, and so have we by listening. Even the caller Mariann from Brooklyn (with the squawking voice) is special because what she says, while she sounds crazy, is valued. Robin is a soft, caring, compassionate, not-to-be-fooled, very intelligent person. Fred is a silent but powerful creative force. Gary is very social, people-oriented, and fast-paced, with an ability to interact with anyone on a variety of subjects. (I still can't believe how he mastered knowing every song and artist ever.) Ronnie is a wild, out-of-the-box, no-boundaries, creative, fun person. Ralph is an intellectual. And the list goes on.

HOMEWORK

1. Complete the exercise outlined in this chapter. Finish any homework that you didn't do from the previous chapter. All that information from those exercises applies to your Magic Dust.

2. Take a sample Myers-Briggs, DiSC, or Enneagram assessment online. Some are free, and I find them accurate. You may need or want a debrief on them, and I highly recommend this as the results leave questions for you about how that information is valuable to you.

3. Based on the results of the above assessments, what traits have you identified as strengths? What areas would you describe as not as strong? What happens when you overuse your strengths so much that others notice?

Note: We will be revisiting Magic Dust throughout the book. Please don't worry if you are uncomfortable with this and haven't been able to identify yours right now.

4
Vision, Mission, Goals, Measures = Behavior

Vision, Mission, Goals, Measures = Behavior

This is a formula that every leader on the planet must have. This is the most powerful leadership process on the planet, and if you do nothing else, please leave this book by completing a vision, mission, goals, measures = behavior document.

A leader must have knowledge about and insight into where they are going. This means every leader at every level. This is the process that will set you free as a leader. It's your time to create what you want, how to do it, and the goals for getting there. I've seen many leaders create this and then come alive in their jobs. A recent graduate of Leadership Journey said his boss asked, "You're doing great — are you going rogue?"

I always say, "Never be an employee; certainly never act like one." Bosses say they want people to make decisions, handle conflict, act like owners, be totally accountable. They want people to show up with a positive attitude and mindset. The boss mentioned above was essentially providing feedback that the Leadership Journey grad was an army of one. She was taking on assignments that she wouldn't normally accept, and he was very happy about this. This is empowering yourself and others to go where they've never gone before.

Vision is a dream or aspiration. Tom Kurtz (Dream Job Tom), an executive coach and colleague once described it as PIE:

- It's **P**ersonal — meaning it links to you and inspires you greatly.
- It's almost **I**mpossible — which means it's difficult and inspires you to go where you've never gone before.
- And it's **E**ternal — it lives on forever; it is your legacy, and it will be going forward even if you're not here.

I like to use four symbols to help us learn, remember, and apply the formula. The first is a telescope. A telescope symbolizes vision because it helps us see way, way out there. It provides us a glimpse into space, which is far away.

A mission can be symbolized by a set of binoculars. A mission is what we are going to do and how we will do it to carry out our vision. A mission brings more clarity, just like binoculars do. It is how you're going to get your vision accomplished. Some call it *the strategy*.

The third symbol is a pair of eyeglasses. Eyeglasses represent our goals. They are our personal goals. They must be 100 percent ours. You cannot wear someone else's glasses. Sometimes with goals, leaders say, "Copy mine." We cannot do that. We must create our own that are specific, measurable, achievable, realistic, and timebound. We need to have specific goals, or we will not have a direction to everyday tasks to reach our vision and mission. It is up to us to monitor and maintain our progress toward each goal. I recommend not more than four or five goals.

The last symbol is that of a tape measure. Are we making progress toward our vision, mission, and goals? And if so, how do we know? We must have measures as leaders. That is why the last symbol is a tape measure.

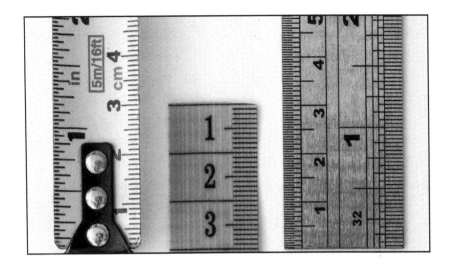

By creating plans that link to these symbols, you will be leading yourself and others on purpose rather than by mistake, chance, or via someone else's plans.

The most important part of the formula v, m, g, m = b is the b part. That is our behavior. Our behavior in everything we do must link to our vision, mission, and goals. If our behavior or our team's behavior is out of alignment with our vision, mission, and goals, then we have an integrity issue between what we say and what we do. This is serious for all leaders.

Let me give an example. If we say we believe in developing people and they are our most important asset, but we pay no attention to people, don't train, mentor, or coach them, and we don't create development plans, then we are saying one thing and doing another. This is not good for any leader at any level. Let's say another leader, for example, claims to be fair in their hiring practices but hires only their friends without regard to others who may be more qualified. This immediately sends a message. We are always sending messages.

All our key processes, such as hiring, rewards, training and development, servicing, coaching, and communication should link to where we are going — and that is our vision, mission, goals, and measures documents. They're not just words on a wall but actual reality for everyone's alignment.

If we give our power to others to create our vision, mission, goals, measures, and behaviors, we are allowing someone else to dictate our lives. If we let them tell us how to apply our Magic Dust, we are allowing our skills, abilities, and talents to be led by someone other than ourselves. I have found this to be the most detrimental thing to a person's career and ultimately life.

What are our vision, mission, goals, measures, and behavior? How will we tie into other people's?

I love Uber because each and every person working with them is an independent contractor. The ability to be free to run and manage your own business is how I see progress in the future. Why? Because there is no one to blame when you don't do well. You can't say it's my boss that made my Uber business fail. In my opinion, more individuals will need to act more like owners of businesses. We need to understand what it means to be self-employed, what it takes to succeed, what hours to work, and when to rest. Do they have rules? Yes. Is anyone working at Uber being forced to? No.

We must be able to influence others. As a leader, this is so very important. How do we influence? My belief is that influence starts with an understanding that we are powerful beyond anything we thought possible. This means that our vision, mission, and goals are very important and should never been minimized. Will they be perfect the first time we create them? Will we achieve the results we are looking for when we announce them? What we need to understand and remember is that leadership is a process not an event, and we must continually refine our vision, mission, and goals and get them where we want them to be.

Our vision at PeopleTek used to be "To help leaders grow and develop." After several years, we changed that statement to reflect our current vision:

"Creating worldwide individual, team, and organizational excellence."

Here are mission statements from some of the world's biggest companies:

American Express
To be the world's most respected service brand.

Microsoft
To empower every person and every
organization on the planet
to achieve more.

Amazon
To be Earth's most customer-centric company,
where customers can find and discover
anything they might want to buy online.

Tesla
Tesla's mission is to accelerate the world's transition to
sustainable energy through increasingly affordable
electric vehicles in addition to renewable
energy generation and storage.

PeopleTek
(Shameless advertising, I know.)
Creating worldwide individual, team,
and organizational excellence.

I interview a lot of individuals who want to improve their careers, their teams, and their organizations. I ask them, "What is your aspiration or vision? Is it written down?" Most answer no to these questions. We require your vision to be written down, as studies years ago showed that leaders who have written goals are 10 to 100 times more successful. So we require it. The bottom line is, do they have one? Where is it? Do others know what it is? Many individuals at all levels say they know where they are going but can't describe their destination.

My advice is to take time to start developing your vision, mission, goals, measures = behavior. Use the template below as a start to setting it up.

Vision, Mission, Goals, Measures = Behaviors (Your Name)			
Vision			
Mission			
Goal	Action	Target Date	Success Measures
Goal 1:			
Goal 2:			
Goal 3:			

Copyright © 2018 PeopleTek Inc. dba PeopleTekCoaching - all rights reserved

WHY HOWARD?

Remember when I said that on any given day you can listen to what Howard does on his show and relate it to leadership? On December 1, 2021, he posted on social media an example of how a vision, mission, goals, and measures = behavior formula can come alive for a person, and how that person or others can either encourage or discourage progress.

Howard gave a perfect example to a woman who was 67 years old and had created a stand-up comedy routine. He said, "Look, I am going to be brutally honest with you and give you feedback because you asked for it. But I want to tell you this. No matter what I tell you, it should never discourage you from living your passion. I was told numerous times how bad I was. And I was bad. However, I did not give up. I kept going. Too often I've seen where people receive feedback and then get discouraged, never to live their life's vision again. I don't want you to have that happen."

To me this is such a great example of true leadership coaching. Why? Because it empowered this person to go where they've not gone before. Howard's vulnerability to admit he was not good in his early years gave her permission to go there also. He used his leadership life to give someone else the courage to live theirs.

I've never met Howard or asked him to discuss this, but I know it clearly without any need for a document or discussion. It is not needed because everything Howard does ties to his vision, which is to make people laugh, have fun, and be happy. His show provides a venue of happiness for the world. He measures this by our listening. By our coming back for more. As long as his team is doing that with the highest quality in mind, they have fun and are happy doing what they love the most.

Many companies I work with labor continually over getting everyone to understand how their role fits in and why they are there. Why? Because they don't really know why they are there. Howard, I am positive, is not doing his job for the money. Yes, the money is important; however, it is and always was a byproduct of a bigger issue for the planet, which is to make us laugh and have fun. He and his team are rewarded greatly for their work. I am not sure what salary everyone makes, but Howard is smart enough to know how critical the team is in his success. That is why they are all doing what they love the most and how they all tie into the vision, mission, goals, and measures. The measures are their wide audience and the feedback they get on what worked and what didn't. Howard and the team, I am sure, listen to the feedback because the shows and wrap-ups reflect that they are discussing what happens in each show. How they could they be better, more authentic, more engaging. I would love to find out the details of how they keep improving the quality of their shows and consistently keep us engaged. All of his key processes, including hiring, rewards, communication, development, and coaching tie to the vision of making us all laugh and have fun while listening.

His vision for entertainment, engagement of the audience, authenticity of each member of the team, creativity in content, and other aspects are clearly understood because of the vision.

Our team works with leaders throughout the world, and we help them establish their vision, mission, goals, measures = behavior documents. Howard lives this in real life. We've already spoken about empowering others. You know his goal is for everyone to laugh, have fun, and be entertained. If the team members are all themselves and authentic, then the show will be outstanding. Why? Because Howard role models being himself, and this gives permission for his team to be themselves as well. Robin can be an authentic Robin. She can talk about her counseling, how she wants to live, what she likes and dislikes, and she can be real. Fred can be behind the scenes making sounds and creating connection points for all of us to the content. Gary can share his views, and everyone can laugh, and he'll take it, so the show can help others find joy and laughter in their days. It is different from sarcasm. It is actual quality control live on air, and Gary gives everyone permission to bash his production in real time. Every team I lead needs to be able to do this, but often they are not capable. Why? Because of our ego. Gary knows he is fine and doesn't need his ego stroked in order to improve his self-esteem. It's for the betterment of the show.

What I am pointing out is that, to succeed, everyone is connected to the vision, mission, goals, measures, and behavior. In our companies, this means that our key processes all need to be linked behaviorally to our vision, mission, and goals. For us, those key processes include

- Hiring
- Rewards
- Communication
- Training
- Coaching
- Content
- Others

Most companies say they have a vision, but they hire based on other factors. Once this happens, and the vision isn't clear, integrity issues can arise. One thing you must say about

Howard's show is that all issues are addressed in real time and live during a broadcast. This means leadership, vision, mission, and goals are live, in action, during the entire show.

Vision, mission, goals, measures = behavior is the single most important leadership formula we all must learn. If we create and implement it like Howard has, we will all be better leaders of our teams and organizations.

Without a vision, there is no direction for an individual, a team, or an organization to follow. You don't even have to sit with Howard for a minute to understand what he is creating. He creates and delivers happiness to millions of listeners. He does this with the help of everyone in the team and the organization. Even the support teams, including technicians, sales, and owners, understand and link to this happiness.

I work with many leaders who are not sure what they are delivering to their customers, and this creates a lot of confusion. Howard makes it simple. Happiness and laughs — that's what he delivers. He does this through exposing people's vulnerability — including his own. He does it by listening and not being afraid of bringing up things that may sound crazy or sophomoric, but they are actually brilliant and insightful.

In addition, if you look at any of the successful people or even aspiring participants Howard interviews, there is one thing we know: they are passionate, and they eat, sleep, and live their vision, mission, and goals. They may not know if their behavior is serving them well, but one thing is sure: they know where they are going. They are not letting anything get in their way.

Even without a template to work from, we can figure out what Howard's vision, mission, goals, measures, and behaviors are …

Let's take a look.

Vision — It has to involve making everyone laugh out loud. Howard wants to keep us engaged and having a fun time. He wants to make our crazy lives easier. The world is hard enough — why not have a Howard to listen to and laugh with, to help us make fun of ourselves and to teach us not to take everything so seriously.

Mission — I interpret Howard's mission to be total honesty with people and pushing the envelope beyond anything on any other media. Howard asks real questions that, yes, may seem immature or childish; however, they hit a real element of our humanity.

How many times we poop; how large our poop is; how often we have sex; what our deepest fears and insecurities are; what our habits are; what we eat; how we sleep; the list of topics covered goes on and on. Howard gets to the root of our humanness.

Goals — 1) Run a funny daily program.
2) Engage the guests by being prepared.
3) Get others on the show to interact, including the guest.

Measures — These probably include tracking the number of listeners, and how popular the show is, and asking whether the show was just plain funny and good.

Behaviors — Here Howard used to be very sarcastic, taking his Magic Dust and overusing it. Was he aware of this? I think not.

But after some self-reflection and seeing a counselor, he was able to see how he was overusing his strength and letting it get in his way. He has even indicated that now he can do entire interviews and not demean his guests in any way. I believe he has calibrated himself nicely and really gets to understand the person he is speaking to, getting into their heart but still making us all laugh.

HOMEWORK

Complete a draft of your personal v, m, g, m = b document. Use our template in this book. Just do it, and don't stop. It will become a working document.

- What are you passionate about achieving?
- What do you think is your key strategy for getting there?
- What are your three to four top goals?
- How will you measure your success?
- What behaviors do you need to get there?

Following is a PeopleTek's template.

Vision, Mission, Goals, Measures = Behaviors (Your Name)

Vision	
Mission	

Goal	Action	Target Date	Success Measures
Goal 1:			
Goal 2:			
Goal 3:			

Copyright © 2018 PeopleTek Inc. dba PeopleTekCoaching. All rights reserved

5
Communication and Listening

When we interview individuals about the traits of their best bosses ever, the first things that usually get raised are a person's communication and listening skills. People want their leaders to hear them. They want to be heard and feel like they've been heard. Let's face it, in all relationships we have a desire to have our messages heard.

The best leaders can clearly send a message and motivate others — and be transparent about what's expected in return.

This is where you will need to spend time building your leadership muscles. It will take a lot of practice.

Here is also where the assessments and information from others can help.

Some examples of communication and listening tools are the same as what we've spoken about already.

Myers-Briggs is a good start. For example, if you are an extrovert and you are dominating every conversation, you can't be listening very well. Likewise, if you are an introvert and not getting your voice heard, you are not speaking up enough. The extroverts (me being one) will dominate if you let them.

In Chapter 3, we narrowed down what type you are, based on the selection of D, I, S, or C. We are going to use that result in this chapter.

As leaders, we need to communicate and listen well.

Keep in mind, we carry our preferred style (D, I, S, or C) with us wherever we go. Let's say we are a D (a Dominant person), and we are speaking to an S (a Steady person); we need to take into consideration our style differences. For example, if we approach the S using a strong D preference, the S may feel like we are being too pushy. Likewise, the D may feel the S is being too easygoing and not moving quickly enough. This is how problems with communication start. The S may say slow down, and the D then asks, "Why don't you want to change?" You can see from this simple example that listening is not being done well on both sides.

We can do the same for I and C, or I and D, and all pairs of styles. Each can and, based on our past experience, will run into issues with style. The question is how aware are you of who you're speaking to? Also ask yourself whether you approach everyone exactly the same way, or whether you adjust when there is a misunderstanding.

In addition to the personality style we are speaking with, we also need to consider our listening ability. Are we listening with judgement, trying to answer before we hear the message, internalizing the message, and becoming defensive about what we are hearing? As leaders we can all work harder on our listening skills. There are a lot of self-reflection techniques available to ensure we are hearing what the other person is saying and verifying we are getting the appropriate message.

There are so many styles, personalities, needs, wants, and desires. Everyone is quirky, and each of us has fabulous gifts. Do we seek to understand the other person? Do we truly want to know how they are, how they operate, what works for them and what doesn't?

Make a list of your team members. How are they different from you? Do they like to be more talkative, or are they quieter? Do you engage them all the same way? What about their interests? How do they prefer to discuss things — from a big-picture perspective or into the details? Are the people concerned about how they come across or are they more directive and goal-focused? Do they like to have a structure and plan, or do they like to live with flexibility and spontaneity?

What kind of assignments do they like? Do you really understand their Magic Dust and the kind of work they will thrive doing? Do they have vision, mission, goals, and measures? Do you know what they are?

WHY HOWARD?

No one on the planet understands effective communication more than Howard. I know that is a bold statement, but I really haven't met them yet if they do. I know Howard goes to counseling and uses those skills on the program with a natural talent, demonstrating to his team and participants that he truly wants to get to know them on a deeper level. There are several reasons his communication skills are so good. One, he cuts beneath the surface of pleasantries and gets to the heart of real-life issues we all face. This builds trust because, although he talks, more importantly he listens. Two, he gets everyone to open up — and this is true communication. Three, he honors everyone's style and approach and caters to their needs. No one was made fun of more than Scott the engineer. Let's face it, engineers are typically a very private, detailed, loyal, and dependable group. Four, Howard brings people out of themselves and gets them to participate. In our program, we use four tools to do this. Howard does it without the tools and by giving feedback right on the spot — live and in your face. I love it! One of our tools is the DiSC assessment (Dominant, Influential, Steady, Conscientious). My guess based on listening to various shows: Howard is a D, Gary is an I, Robin is an SC, and Fred a C or SC. This shows a balance in the team and gives quite a view of how effectively they operate together.

Communication. This is where Howard is a master. He is the best interviewer because he relates to his audience, whether it is one person or many. He listens and then comments. He asks great questions. He goes deep without flinching. He understands that everyone is different, and he communicates to them directly. I agree with a statement he made in his book — over time he has become a better interviewer. I don't listen to his show all the time or for many hours like I did in the 90s. But what I do notice these days is that he is much more respectful in his approach. He can get the same results and still be respectful. That is the key. At PeopleTek, we always talk about healthy, honoring, and respectful conflict. Well, this idea starts with communication. Howard is able to build a relationship. He focuses on the other person and their needs. He gets to know them on a personal level. This is what makes communication so important. It is about how you relate to others. Howard can do this with introverts, extroverts, intuitives, and anal-retentives. He truly wants to know people, and this shows in how he deals with others. He is direct when he needs to be and backs off when he needs to as well.

I think this is because, ultimately, he is an introvert. When it comes to Myers-Briggs, I'm usually not far off with my guesses. He is probably an INTP or INFP. I would love to type him more officially.

Considering who are we speaking to and what we want them to know, without trying to control the audience, gives us the power to have fun, let go, and be free. We all learn, grow, and transform when we are better communicators. I find Howard knows exactly what to ask so we all benefit from his questions to the guest. Time and time again, I've seen him ask questions of his guest that I was thinking. That is the key: having these questions ready and not being afraid to go there. This means that Howard checks in with himself on points that make him feel uncomfortable and plays with the guest in their style. He has diversity and inclusion mastered because he does this with guests who are Black, white, Hispanic, male, female, and so on.

Howard is not afraid to learn from others. This trait makes a great communicator. I've only seen him become uncomfortable once, from what I can pick up. I mean to ask him about it. He was speaking with Robert Plant of Led Zeppelin. I think, ultimately, they are alike, and it scared Howard to go too deep with someone so similar.

Howard's interviews — and his ability to get others to feel both comfortable and vulnerable — are masterful. He uses multiple approaches to listening. In our Leadership Journey, we use a tool that measures if you are an empathic, appreciative, discerning, evaluative, or comprehensive listener. Each of these types focuses on a different listening approach.

Empathic — Focuses on the feelings of others

Appreciative — Focuses on how the other person looks and the image they convey

Discerning — Focuses on what the person is saying

Evaluative — Focuses on making certain inferences about the information given

Comprehensive — Focuses on bringing in multiple sources to understand what is being said with nonverbal cues, such as body language and so on

Howard uses all these approaches. Again, you can listen on any day, select an interview, and hear him in action. For example, he interviewed the rock group Metallica about their ballad "Nothing Else Matters," written by James Hetfield. Howard used every form of listening to get the band to open up. What was revealed was magical for the audience and the band. Why? Because, yet again, the moment gave us permission to be our authentic selves. Howard asked James if he wrote the song because he was missing his girlfriend at the time. James said yes.

Howard then asked how their audience reacted, if they resisted this love song, and if they threw it out because of the style. James said no. They were totally surprised at the reaction to their song. Apparently, they found that the Hells Angels were using it as a theme song, as were couples for their weddings, and other listeners were using it for many acts of appreciation.

If Howard hadn't connected all the dots with his communication, listening and questioning, we would not have benefitted from hearing this. What we can learn from James opening up is that we can be ourselves. We don't have to apologize. We need to communicate from our hearts even if others may disapprove; we need to be the creative leaders we were destined to be.

Where is communication working for you? Where is it not? Can you get deeper into understanding the people you work with and for? Now that you understand yourself a little more, what is it you wish to find out about others? Can you speak to them in their style?

HOMEWORK

Go back to your vision, mission, goals, measures = behavior documents.

- My first question is, have you shared your vision, mission, goals, measures = behavior document with anyone? If so, how was it received?
- If you haven't done so, please, even if it's just in draft form, create this document and present it to two to five people.
- Please write down their reactions and their feedback about it.

6
Clarity

Clarity occurs when you combine the skills of vision, mission, goals, measures = behaviors, and you create and implement a plan that has all of the elements of roles, responsibilities, and actions tied to it. Clarity is the part of communication that links the reality of what you are doing to the words you speak. This link creates alignment. It is also where we and other leaders sometimes get tripped up. For example, we may say we believe that "people" are our most important asset. Saying that and behaving like that are two different things. Many companies I've worked with try their best to link a written plan to their words and actions. Too often their processes don't line up. They have written statements on the walls, their websites, and their hiring documents, but then they don't live and breathe the statements in reality. For example, if you say you are someone who believes in "people" but at the same time provide no alignment with your key processes, then you are out of alignment, and clarity in the organization will be poor. You have values but you are not living them on a daily basis and may not even know it. This is an integrity problem for you and for your organization. If we believe that certain skills are important, but we don't hire for them, we are not linking words with actions. This makes things very unclear, and people don't know how to follow. The key processes that must be aligned are hiring, rewards, communication, operational and customer support, training, education, and coaching, to name a few. Every person's development plan in the company must link to where they are going.

Clarity includes specific instructions on where you are going as a leader. It requires alignment and getting the communication out to align as team-specific tasks that must get done to gain momentum as a team.

As a leader, this is an area that I work on the most. Why? Because clarity is my weakest area, based on feedback, and it links to accountability. Clarity is about filling in the blanks, outlining the why, gaining alignment with others and how they see things. It's about searching for mutual understanding. So many times, I've thought I communicated the next steps clearly only to find out later that my team needed more details and a clearly defined plan. If I had been more inquisitive and hadn't wanted to move on so quickly, I may have uncovered this sooner.

There is an assessment called The Work of Leaders (Wiley Publishing). This tool is used to measure how effective leaders perform the behaviors required to carry out their plans. After researching leaders in many disciplines over several years, the developers of the tool found it necessary to be good in three primary areas: Vision, Alignment, and Execution. We may be good at vision and not so good at alignment and execution. Alignment requires us to get into the details of what we are trying to accomplish, and execution requires us to be very good at taking a task, staying focused, and implementing it. My advice would be to surround yourself with individuals who have strengths in areas that complement yours. Based on what I've observed, Howard does a very good job at this with his team and support staff.

WHY HOWARD?

While I've never seen Howard's vision, mission, goals, measures = behavior, we can all witness how he is gaining clarity. He does this through live coaching. He takes what he has and, on live radio, aligns with the values and beliefs he feels are required to operate on his team.

For years, I heard him coach people who were on his team, like Scott the engineer. Howard would give feedback by teasing. Yes, this would be considered sarcasm and not acceptable in "professional" environments in the "real world." But the great thing about Howard's show is that his team members were able to laugh at themselves and their habits.

- Gary, with his programming shortcomings
- Robin, with her private nature
- Fred, with his private and weird nature

All of this is alignment with clarity. Howard creates this alignment live. He would probably say, "I think Mike is nuts, and I was just doing a show." This is what is tremendous and why no one can take offense like we do in our companies — because Howard is so real and authentic. He also never fires anyone. He gives feedback and multiple chances.

I tuned in recently to a clip that was reposted on Howard's Facebook page. In the clip, Howard was asking Memet why he was so upset and gloomy. Was it because of the feedback he had gotten from Howard about his PowerPoint presentation? Memet said, "Yes. All I got was a red strike through it from you [Howard]." Howard said, "Yes, I didn't like it." So they debriefed the PowerPoint in front of everyone. Memet was hurt because he'd spent three weeks working on it. The presentation, while creative, had some issues that rubbed Howard's values the wrong way. It had some things in it that Howard felt should not be done, such as bashing Oprah and Ellen Degeneres. What I love about the interaction is that everyone got a chance to provide feedback to Memet. Memet also got to share his feelings of discouragement with the team. It doesn't even matter if the PowerPoint was used or not. The bottom line is that this is what needs to happen in all companies. An open, honest dialogue and alignment of what will work and what may not work. We need to ask how does this fit into our company culture, and what doesn't work?

I am very proud of Howard and his team for showing this example of leadership and teamwork in public. This is how you keep relationships and build trust.

This does not happen in many companies. Companies often make a hire, sometimes poorly, and then provide no coaching or feedback, and then say the new hire is doing badly. Howard brings every conversation into the public view. We could all do this. Why don't we? Because we are afraid of getting fired or sued or of not looking good. So we just do worse and keep it hidden.

I was married for 33 years. I had a great wife, but we didn't talk about anything or make any progress toward change. We said we loved each other, but our behaviors didn't link to those words. My new partner, Wilda, is not afraid to say anything, argue in any direction, and laugh after we finish. She is not afraid to call me on anything that she perceives is off base. We've broken up 18 times, but we're together now, and we finally know we care about each other.

Howard does the same. Howard shares of himself about his insecurities, values, beliefs, habits, behavior (good and bad), likes and dislikes. This makes it easier for us to know him and relate. It also makes it easier when you know that someone knows how to communicate, handle conflict, align behavior with vision, and show trust: actions that impact so many leadership outcomes. The same is true for any successful organization or team.

Howard has very low turnover if any, and high loyalty and dedication — and a number-one show running for how many years? Howard speaks his mind and encourages others to do the same.

Howard is vulnerable and talks about his weaknesses. He encourages others to do the same. He wants all his team's strengths and weaknesses exposed.

> He asks tough questions.
> He demands perfection.
> He laughs at mistakes.

His behavior links 100 percent to what he says he's about.

This makes his team, organization, and company culture great.

All of us would like a company that runs like that. If we were able to achieve that, there would be no surprises, and our wins would be so much greater.

Sometimes we need to observe others for clarity. In a recent show, Howard interviewed Mick Jagger. He asked Mick how he came up with his moves. Mick said that he watched others, like Prince and Elvis. He said he observed their styles, took the best skills from each of them, especially the art of timing, and worked these skills into his act. To me, this is a wonderful way to use someone else's Magic Dust and bring more clarity to discovering or validating ours.

Learning from others. This is another way to gain clarity.

By listening to Howard, we can also learn nuggets of gold like this one.

HOMEWORK

Alignment is your integrity to yourself. You set a vision, mission, goals, and measures into action. Are you aligned with them? What alignment means is that if you have a vision and mission that lead you in a direction, you must align your behaviors to match what you are attempting to achieve. To do this, you must be an observer of your behaviors. Consider the following:

1. Where are you spending your time? Are you putting time into activities that bring you closer to your outlined vision, mission, and goals? Are you in a role that aligns best to what it is you have outlined in your vision and mission?

2. For example, if you said you want to be in a role that uses your presentation skills, but you keep avoiding presentations, then you are saying one thing and doing another. Look for examples where you are living in alignment with what you desire.

3. Are you spending money in areas that also don't align? If so, your homework is to make adjustments in these areas and align your behavior to your stated vision, mission, and goals.

7
Accountability

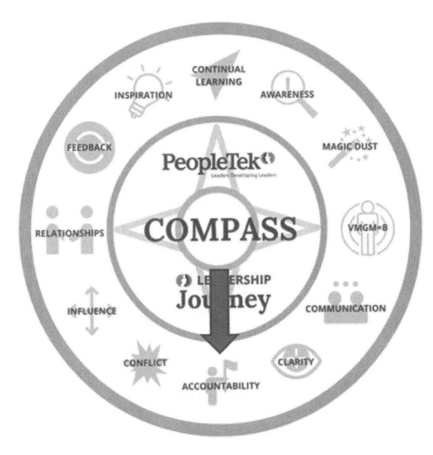

Accountability was, and still is, my greatest weakness, and it links directly to clarity. How do I know it's my greatest weakness? My team tells me. The funny thing is that when I do hold others accountable, after much discussion, then I am told I am too hard. Everyone wants accountability until it's pointed at them. I remember one occasion when I had gotten my 360 feedback. This is when your team members, bosses, peers, colleagues, and customers all give you feedback on how you're doing. This was year two, and I had already received feedback a year earlier. I was told in year two that I had gotten much better; however, I still needed to improve more in holding others accountable. I said, "They just don't get it." The coach debriefing the feedback said, "I think you're getting a little defensive, aren't you?" I screamed at him, "No!"

We both laughed. Feedback can be a tough thing to handle.

Howard is a master at giving it because it's live on the radio. If he needs to tell someone that he is frustrated with something, you know it right away. He may yell or say it over and over, but you know it that day. I have heard him do this repeatedly on his show. If it's Scott, Fred, Ronnie, Gary, Robin, or anyone else, Howard is relentless. I know his team doesn't love it, but they love Howard and know this is part of the show. They trust each other more because of this. If you read the book *The Five Dysfunctions of a Team*, you will see that feedback is crucial to a team's performance.

When someone on Howard's show is not behaving according to his expectations, he openly shares the issue with the audience. This is absolutely fabulous. While at times he is sarcastic (not a good thing), the issue of openly discussing behavior is terrific. Howard is not afraid to have conflict. As author Patrick Lencioni states in *The Five Dysfunctions of a Team*, one of the major areas that destroys trust is talking behind someone's back instead of giving them feedback directly.

See the optimal level:

Trust none of the time   Trust all the time

The point is we are all different in how we approach trust, and we fall somewhere on the line depending on who we are dealing with and what we need to share. For example, unless we really trust ourselves and others, there are things we will not share because we are afraid of the repercussions. Howard is not afraid to share almost anything. He shares about his health, his phobias, his parents, some details about his wife, but never anything about his daughters. He also wants his guests to share openly about their experiences and be real with the audience.

Robin, Gary, Ronnie, and others have openly shared on the show things that many people would not. That is what makes everything special. They are real. They are vulnerable. For example, we know Robin's history of bad things that happened to her as a child. She has done so much to work on herself, and this is evident. The best thing is that she is an example of how as individuals we can have these things in our past. Yes, they hurt, but we can move forward with our careers and lives and be very successful.

Gary has a similar story to me. I only heard parts of it on one show, but he mentioned his mom and his relationships with his wife and family. I had a similar situation, and it was not easy. The good thing is Howard's team shares openly on SiriusXM Radio for all their listeners to hear and benefit from. This gives everyone a chance to be open and vulnerable.

WHY HOWARD?

Howard demands perfection. He wants all of us to laugh. He brings up problems with quality on the radio, including when technology isn't working well, when Gary or others are not up to par, and when people are late. Or he'll discuss their quirks of communication, Robin's and Fred's behavior, and it goes on and on. The show is made of this kind of thing, and so you can trust Howard because if it is evident, he will speak openly on air and bring problems to light. If someone overuses their strength in a weird way, Howard doesn't let it go by, such as when Memet was bragging about his IQ. Clearly Memet is smart, but when anyone overuses their IQ or thinks they are better because of it, or they are using their IQ to the point where it creates issues for others, Howard brings this to light. I love it because it is what all effective leaders need to do. Sometimes Howard is sarcastic, and that is a danger zone to be very careful of. He has a comedy show, so it is difficult to stay away from sarcasm; however, Howard is a master at making it actually real and not overly sarcastic. I would love to discuss this balance at some point with him.

Sometimes Howard can go into the danger zone. I think this is where he is much more professional and honoring now than he has been in the past. He is right in his book — he has improved! How do I know? He says it best: I can still get my point across and not demean others. I can still give them feedback where we all learn and grow. At PeopleTek, we call this "Feedback in a Healthy, Honoring, Respectful Manner." Sometimes on the *Howard Stern Show*, this gets out of control. There is a point of unhealthy conflict, and sometimes the show can go there. Howard now recognizes it more clearly. You want this more than no conflict. Why? Because with no conflict, there is little to no growth. Overall, Howard is not afraid of how others will respond. He'd rather address a problem than let it go unresolved. Most of the world would rather let it go and not deal with the uncomfortable feelings that are created.

We will never make progress as a society unless in a healthy, honoring way we can provide our perspectives and listen without reacting in an unhealthy manner.

Howard is actually teaching us how to be better emotionally. How to show up and have a conversation about uncomfortable issues. Sex and money are the toughest ones, and he handles sexuality most often. For many years people said he was degrading to women. I bet you can't find one woman who's ever been on the show who said she felt that way. He respects women greatly, and you can tell by the way he and Robin communicate and treat each other.

You can turn Howard on almost any day and experience accountability in action. In fact I turned on the radio and right away there was a segment with the team getting all over Benjy's behavior. He was acting up in a restaurant and being me, me, me oriented. This is not great for the team. His behavior involves the perception of others. Effective teams can openly discuss the perception of others. Howard and the team were giving Benjy feedback. They were a little tough; however, it's better to give the feedback than to not talk about it. This is leadership in action. Howard exposes the issue, and then everyone on the team comments. You might say this wastes time; however, from working with teams for many years, I see what really wastes time is keeping everyone in the dark. Yes, Benjy may never change; however, you can't say he doesn't now have information about his impact on his coworkers. Again, Howard would not hold back from anyone, whether it's Gary, Fred, Robin, Ronnie, Memet, Benjy ... and even himself. By Howard's showing his vulnerabilities in public, he gives permission to everyone to do the same.

I love that Howard is open and authentic, and that he shares his vulnerability. I can't thank him enough for this.

HOMEWORK

1. If you're leading others, please cite examples of both good and poor behavior being observed. Look for specific examples of how this behavior is getting in the way of performance toward the stated vision, mission, goals, and measures.

2. If you are not leading a team and need to give yourself feedback, here is your homework: Observe again if you are not living in alignment with your stated vision, mission, and goals. What is getting in the way? Procrastination? You need to either hire a coach or obtain a mentor to hold you accountable. Or JUST hold YOURSELF accountable and change your behavior. As homework, I want you to list what behaviors are taking you away from your stated vision, mission, and goals.

8
Conflict
(Without Conflict There Is No Leadership)

This quotation is from a fellow coach, Tom Kurtz. I'm not sure where he heard it, so I will give him the credit. I've been using it for years. "If you are not stretching, you are not growing. If you are not growing, you are not leading."

Howard embodies this better than anyone. Not only with his staff, but also with his audience. He empowers us to go where we've not gone before. This makes all of us better leaders. He inspires us to go beyond our comfort zones, to listen, and to share our vulnerability and our humanness.

Many team members are artificially "nice" to each other. Many families are this way. I can do this too much too. I hold back even though I know in my heart someone is wrong.

Many of our families are divided over politics and political mindsets — this applies to me as well. I had a relative ask me, "Why do you want unrealistic goals?" when I mentioned world-wide health insurance for everyone. She felt that because this is unattainable, we should keep what we have and not strive for such lofty goals. I believe that if we have a desire, we can achieve it. And I just don't like her reasoning that everything needs to stay the same.

For example, if we charged 10 cents for every container that is created in factories, we could potentially fund the Health Care for All initiative. I just know that if we all have a goal, and it is simple health care FOR EVERYONE on the planet, at some point I believe we can achieve it. Now, do I speak about it? Do I fight for my point until I drop? No, I give up.

This is where I believe my accountability ends, and where Howard's doesn't. He is not afraid to use his platform to make this a better planet. You may recall him shouting, "WHAT IS THE BIG DEAL IN WEARING A MASK?"

WHY HOWARD?

Howard is the master of conflict, and this ties to accountability. Howard's ability to address a conflict is what makes him an outstanding example of leadership. Even when he is not right on a topic, he will at least address behavior that is not proper with his team members and others. He does this sometimes in a messy way, but he does it. He is not afraid to speak his mind. He is not afraid to ask tough questions. He is not afraid to take risks with his behavior. He is not afraid of who will like him and who won't.

He engages in conflict directly on the live show. What better way to teach than to have all of us listening.

If you had a team and everyone listened to how you handled situations, there would be so much less hall talk. Yes, we all know what hall talk is — when leadership pulls someone aside and talks to them about their behavior. Howard is purposefully giving feedback live on the radio to each of his staff. Ronnie the limo driver can be a pain sometimes with his behavior. So can Gary, Robin, Fred ... So can Howard, and so can I. We all can — and that is the point.

Our greatest strengths often show up as clear areas in need of development. That's right: our Magic Dust is the thing we will get called out on the most. Why? Because at times we overuse it, and that is what trips us up most.

Fred being too quiet and reflective. Robin being too deep and intuitive. Gary being too enthusiastic. Howard being too picky or healthy ... These strengths turn into our Achilles heel. This is so very important. Even if you burn the entire book, keep this one part: please, please find out your Magic Dust. Learn to use it with the proper motivation and understand what happens when you overuse it.

A recent episode of the show offered an example of initiating conflict. The team was discussing talk-show host Katie Couric.

She was recently a guest host on *Jeopardy!*, following Alex Trebek's death. Suddenly the media said there were concerns about her guest role because she didn't support former president Trump and was outspoken against Republican decisions and policies. Howard and Robin began to talk without reservation about the double standard that exists regarding these issues. Howard said the controversy was due to gender bias, and he pointed to several other examples of men disagreeing with the same leader — and they were still on television. What could the reason be for the concerns other than gender bias? Howard is willing to step up and raise the conflict, which can at the very least start the conversation. Again, without conflict there is no leadership

For close to 30 years at PeopleTek, we've been helping leaders understand this idea, and we haven't met one leader who doesn't have Magic Dust but also overuse it to the detriment of themselves or others. My great friend the late Dr. Abe Fischler said it best when he attended the Leadership Journey at 80 years old: "If I had known this information about myself, I would have handled things so very differently at different stages of my life. My decisions may have been very different and more impactful."

What I know is this: if you're reading this, you are ready to find out. The leaders we graduate say they save 82-plus hours per person per year by having this knowledge.

Howard makes an entire show out of helping and coaching others on this issue. We all need a Howard to point this out for us as a coach, mentor, friend, and most importantly as a boss.

HOMEWORK

Outline some discomfort you are experiencing with attaining your vision, mission, and goals. Note, if you are not experiencing discomfort, then you probably need to push yourself a little outside of your comfort zone.

An example of resisting pushing yourself is if you wish to take on a sales role and earn additional income or try a leadership role but never apply for these positions. You are probably making excuses because you are comfortable and don't want to experience an uncomfortable feeling. There are many examples of things we resist. Let's say you've resisted creating your vision, mission, and goals document. Why?

What is preventing you from writing down your desires? It could be you are afraid to make a mistake. We must get rid of that belief and change it to "I am fine if I make a mistake." You can feel sad, but do not let the feeling prevent you from achieving your dreams. A major step toward this is to create your vision, mission, goals, measures, and behaviors.

9
Influence

We need to use all areas of our process to exert our influencing skills. We are all part of a team, so how do we get our vision to come alive? How do we impact others to accomplish what we, our customers, and other constituents need? There are many tools and behaviors to influence. In some way, all the previous chapters here impact our ability to influence others. If we don't influence others, our vision will not be achieved.

Influencing skills and behavior can generate the most powerful argument for those who think that "everyone is a leader." I've heard before that only those who wield significant influence are leaders. Or only those who make major things happen are leaders. This couldn't be further from the truth. The fact is we are all leaders. Every person on the planet. All the tools we've provided during this COMPASS process show us how we can make our influence come alive.

In fact, it starts with our awareness of our strengths and weaknesses. This awareness leads us to the discovery of our Magic Dust. By now you should have determined some areas in which you are special. Now the challenge is to find the confidence to use those skills, abilities, and talents in what you do every day. For example, if you find yourself to be a "motivator" with your Magic Dust, where are you applying this skill? If you find yourself to be a detailed, analytical person, how are you using these skills daily to help yourself, your job, and others? If you find yourself to be a results-oriented, get-it-done person, how are you making those traits come alive? I know that I am good with relationships and inspiring others. I know that if I use these skills properly, other people will rise to the occasion and accomplish great things. I get a chance to apply this every day in the work I do.

What about you? How are you doing what you're skilled in every day? Using your special skills, abilities, and talents is having your Magic Dust come alive. This is where true influence is felt and valued. We all have the ability to influence others in different ways. What is so interesting is that others can see and feel our Magic Dust in action sometimes better than we can. In doing feedback sessions, it is not uncommon for individuals to downplay how easy certain influencing skills come to them. This is because they are totally aligned with a role that matches their Magic Dust, and the ability to see their influence is obvious to everyone.

There are so many other areas of the COMPASS that relate to influencing others. For example, vision, mission, goals, measures = behavior. This formula can influence others in many ways and actually do it quite quickly. The more we are all aligned with where we are going, the easier it is to influence others because they have participated and already agree they want to be part of the formula, and their Magic Dust is appreciated.

In a Mastermind session, we recently heard three examples of where and how to influence others.

The perfect example of influence came from Lee, who shared how his team and Karthik's downstream team rallied together to solve a problem. They had a similar v, m, g, m = b and used their shared vision to help their customers by solving a production issue. Recognizing and rewarding those who played a part in the solution are great ways to build unity.

Tamara shared how she influences by having genuine conversations with others in which she seeks and values their input. Understanding why people act the way they do is key to leading well and finding common ground.

Finally, Boyd shared his experience with a difficult person in his new workplace.

I appreciate each of you who shared great wisdom, including the following advice:

1. Figure out what motivates the other person and what's in it for them. Speak to them in a way so that they'll listen.

2. Have regular status meetings to see where things are and get input.

3. Remember, long-term relationships take patience.

4. It's not about you. When someone rejects your idea or relationship, it's almost never because of you. Don't take the rejection personally.

5. Align your vision, mission, goals, measures = behavior for maximum influence and success.

WHY HOWARD?

The reason I say Howard is an expert at influencing others is evident not only in his success, but also in the extent to which others follow him. In addition, his legacy of laughter and joy cannot be ignored. Whether you like him or not, Howard is a master influencer.

He influences using a variety of tactics. One, he is clear about his vision, mission, and goals. Two, he is a master communicator. Three, he is a leader of a successful team. I know he meets with his team daily to set their work in motion. I know they have creative meetings. I know they give feedback, and any unit that supports them is also given feedback. All behavioral issues on the show get discussed live. Whether this is Robin, Gary, Fred, Ronnie, Sal, Benjy, Richard, Memet, or any member of the team, all will be discussed in front of everyone. They are totally transparent with each other. That kind of behavior is needed for effective communication and teams. This approach empowers them to be open, honest, and direct. This builds trust, which is the foundation of teamwork.

Howard communicates. He is vulnerable and open, listens, and is direct. You also get the impression he cares. You learn what he cares about. He shares this with finesse and ease, and others want to be part of that experience. That is influence. He is able to get others to communicate, open up, be vulnerable, care, and listen. He is the role model that sets the tone. This gives others permission to do the same. That is influence at the highest level. Others want to copy his approach. This has been cited numerous times throughout the years of his program. Most important of all, Howard gets us to tune in over and over again. The highest compliment ever is that we come back over and over for years. Who can be a better influencer than someone who accomplishes that?

If you look at Howard's behavior as it relates to influence, he is involved in every point. Let's take a few examples of his behavior.

Self-Reflection: He influences us by looking inside himself and permitting us to take that journey as well. He sees a psychologist. If it is good enough for Howard, it's good enough for everyone. He gives examples on the show of how self-reflection has hurt him or made him a better person.

Magic Dust: No one uses the special skills, abilities, and talents of others better than Howard.

He digs deep in his interviews. Listen to past interviews, and you will see how he gets the guest to feel special and be heard, while helping the audience to learn. We learn by his probing. If we as leaders could be half as good as coaches of our teams, they would feel so honored to work for us. They would know we really cared. For example, asking Billy Joel why he would not write songs with others. Asking Paul McCartney about his relationship with John Lennon and the other Beatles. Or probing Robin about her past traumas, Gary about his relationship with his mom, Fred about his introversion. Tackling all of these issues is what an effective leader should do.

Howard is able to pick on our quirky behavior. He does this by poking at things in our personality that make us weird and unique. This poking can sometimes go too far and be viewed as cruel and distasteful. We can also take this too far if we are leaders. (In the corporate world, we could also get sued. However, that is a problem with corporate America.) We need to acknowledge and trust each other that we won't use feedback or information we receive from an individual who is being open and vulnerable to hurt that person's career, financial rewards, promotions, and so on. The reason we are doing the feedback and discussion is to be a better team, deliver better results, and service our customers more effectively.

Most of the time, Howard is poking fun at what we are overusing and gets in our way. He has even brought out the best in the Wack Pack. For example, Mariann is loud and can sound obnoxious. She is overusing her passion and extroversion. But by Howard teasing her and Fred "playing the bird" (a loud noise that sounds like a bird) when Mariann calls in, they allow her to speak from a large platform. Yes, some of it is sarcastic; however, they all light up our lives, with Howard highlighting their weirdness and respecting it.

HOMEWORK

I have a saying: "I want to be physically, mentally, emotionally, spiritually, sexually, financially, and relationally the healthiest in the cemetery." The spark can come initially from an external factor, such as a book (hopefully, *The Leadership Lessons of Howard Stern*), a workshop, a coach ... but finding success in our career, and living our passions and dreams must come both internally and externally. We can help ourselves and others, for sure, but we must do our own work. It cannot be avoided. It may mean we also need a formal coach or mentor to keep us moving forward.

For homework, do the following:

1. Identify one to two people in your life who might act as a mentor to you.

2. Have a meeting with them to discuss your goals.

3. Ask them to be a mentor to you.

4. Identify someone in your life whom you can mentor. If you are already leading a team, create and implement a development plan for every person who works for you. This plan should include helping them create and implement their vision, mission, goals, measures, and behavior documents.

10
Relationships

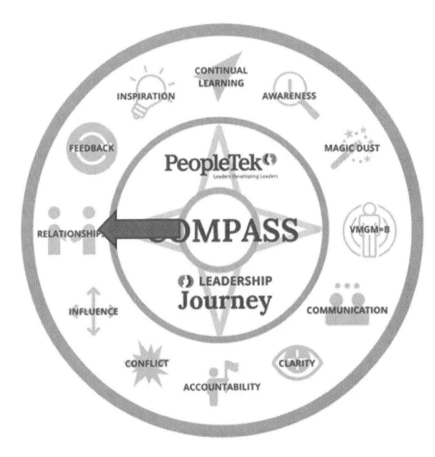

I believe that this point on the COMPASS is crucial for our success. After an assignment or role is completed, the relationships we built during that time go on and on, or end.

Many leaders understand this from the start, and they use their relationship skills to get things done. Yes, like all the other points on the COMPASS, building relationships comes naturally to some. To others, not quite. I am one for whom this skill comes naturally. I like speaking with people. I like to get them involved in what I do. I need them to accomplish my goals. I want to understand their vision, mission, goals, and measures so we can help each other in our work and lives. I believe our lives and careers can improve when we support each other to achieve our legacy. Each person being important, unique, special, and no one being any better than others, we are all special. Everyone's legacy is important in different ways. We meet so many people along the way, and it's these people you will remember after your vision, mission, goals, and measures are completed or well on their way.

I've had opportunities to work with so many wonderful people. And it is these people who enabled me to learn and grow as a person, colleague, and business owner.

If you are in a leadership role and have responsibilities, make a list of the people you work with. Find out what they are about and how they prefer to show up. What can you do to help them? How can you all get wins on your vision, mission, and goals? Many people will say they don't know the answers to these questions. Well, then maybe they just want to be heard.

We've gone through many tools and instruments like Myers-Briggs, Enneagram, and DiSC. With these in mind, think about who you are speaking to. Are you speaking to them in your style, or theirs? Are you giving them what they need in order to be successful in their job? If you use these tools and others and take an honest look at how you show up at work, you will get better at these skills. Don't stop with just one tool. In our program we use five, plus a 360 feedback assessment. There are never too many assessments to give you data.

I remember reading Walter Isaacson's biography of Steve Jobs. Isaacson wrote that when Steve was ill, he asked a previous head of HR whether she thought he had learned how to deal with others better. In the past he'd had very poor relationships with coworkers and people who worked for him. The HR head told Steve he had learned to deal with people and was so much better at it. You see, even after all he'd accomplished and invented, and all the changes he'd brought to our world, it was people whom Steve felt were important.

WHY HOWARD?

I believe building relationships is Howard's biggest strength. Yes, I have a man crush. Get over it and read on, so you can learn something and become a better leader.

Howard builds relationships. He uses his communication and listening skills to home in on a connection so that you feel he is your friend, and you can call him for advice or just talk, and he will listen. These new skills discovered after years of therapy make his relationship skills even more powerful. First, let's start with Robin. Robin is loyal, dedicated, patient, and — yes — brilliant. She is soft-spoken, articulate, refined, well-educated, intuitive, and deep, and she brings her brilliance in the exact opposite way that Howard does in order to complement his skills. Her role with Howard is perfect because she can see things and tell him what she observes, and he listens deeply to her advice. She sees things before they happen because she is — if I were to use some of our tools and type her, I would probably see she is Howard's opposite in personality. This is why Howard is a master. He understands the concept of someone's Magic Dust; he creates a common bond and then works tirelessly to create a team, so everyone works together.

He does this with Fred who is extremely introverted. From my experience living with introverts, they like their alone time, are very reflective, and like to be behind the scenes. They are usually very deep thinkers. Howard knows how to let Fred be himself, use his Magic Dust, and help make the show great. Howard does the exact same with Gary, Richard, Benjy, Ronnie, and all the others.

They are friends for life as well as coworkers.

I guarantee, if Howard has a falling out, the person involved is given every opportunity to make it right with Howard and the show.

I've only seen Howard uncomfortable with a relationship once. That was a few years ago when he interviewed Robert Plant. Not that Howard did anything wrong. I'm not sure, but I felt both of them were so similar that Howard was uncomfortable. By similar, I mean they shared a sense of creativity, influence, style, and intellect. I'm not sure this is what made Howard uncomfortable, but I noticed a difference in him during the interview that I hadn't observed before in all the years I've listened.

HOMEWORK

List three relationships in your life — two good ones and one not so good. What do you think helps make the relationships good? What makes the other not work?

Do these people know about your vision, mission, and goals?

How, if at all, do these relationships impact your vision, mission, goals, and measures?

If you have direct reports or peers who work with you, do they know about your vision, mission, and goals? Are they supportive of you achieving them? If not, why?

11
Feedback

In 1988, I received feedback. I was leading a large IT department for a financial services company. My direct reports and key internal customers said I was visionary, motivating, inspiring, good with all my relationships, and achieved results, but I had a flaw. I was wishy-washy and didn't hold others accountable for their behavior. As a leader, this feedback devasted me, as I didn't know what was causing my problem. I asked HR what to do, and they said they didn't know. I hired a woman named Dr. Carol Hutton, who came in and worked with me. She showed me how my behavior was creating these impressions. I asked her to work with our team, and for almost two years she helped us transform from one of the lowest scoring company Value Survey results to the best in the IT department. The rest is history. I loved coaching so much that I got certified in various tools and processes, quit corporate life (Jimmy Kimmel's father, Jim, helped me go part-time for about six months in my then-current position), and started PeopleTek — working with people in technologies. A buddy of mine said, "Mike, make it a Tek, as you will be working with everyone." (He meant that I would appeal to any industry not just information technology organizations.) Best decision I've made! Thank you, Tom Kurtz, aka Dream Job Tom.

I am telling this story here in the chapter on feedback because feedback is fabulous. Yes, it hurts; yes, it can be devastating, but it can also be beneficial — it was for me for the rest of my life. I learned to adjust my behavior and not be controlled by it.

The thing about feedback that is so powerful is that it comes from our strengths. Yes, our strengths, if overused, are our Achilles' heel. Our powerful Magic Dust, if it is overused, gets in our way and becomes our greatest problem to overcome.

I want each of you to ask for feedback. If you have a formal way to get feedback, all the better. If not, please start with the COMPASS. Give each person you've chosen to give you feedback a blank copy of the COMPASS in this book. Please ask friends, family members, coworkers, and especially bosses to rate you from 1 to 5 in each area, with 5 being the best and 1 representing a need for improvement. Tell them you would be very appreciative. This is your start to understanding blind spots in the way you show up. The feedback will provide you with information that is important for your career and your future.

If you receive negative feedback, it doesn't mean you did anything wrong. Generally, our negative feedback comes from overusing our strength. For example, if we are detail-oriented and analytical, we may get feedback that we are too picky and sometimes anal. We may get feedback that we take too long to make a decision. The reason for this kind of feedback is that we may be overusing what we think of as our strengths. If you recall, this idea connects to our Magic Dust. Generally, when overused, our Magic Dust can get in our way and in others' way.

Sometimes we can be awesome with ideas and creativity, but we might be so good in these areas that we don't consider all the ramifications and are not as good at implementing the ideas. Sometimes we are great with people but become too nice and afraid to address problems with them. In over 30 years of providing feedback and helping others, I haven't met anyone on the planet who doesn't have wonderful Magic Dust. But at times we all have a tendency to overuse it. The more aware we become of our Magic Dust and our colleagues' Magic Dust, the better leaders, managers, and coaches we become. All of this must start with us. We must lead ourselves before we lead anyone else.

Stop, get some feedback, and take a look at yourself. See if what they are saying makes sense. Match it to some of the tools I've suggested, like Myers-Briggs, DiSC, and Enneagram. See if the tools relate to your strengths. Determine if your feedback links to overusing your Magic Dust.

WHY HOWARD?

The other reason I mention it to you is that Howard uses giving and receiving feedback as a tool to create and carry out his program. Howard discusses openly how perceptions of others are interpreted by himself and others, including his team, his audience, almost everyone. Howard takes feedback and magnifies it. He uses his platform to discuss perceptions of behavior. This is masterful. He does it with finesse. Some listen and make adjustments; others don't. He takes the perceptions that many hold about a subject and brings them to life. He makes us laugh about them; he makes some cry, at least internally.

The thing I love about feedback is that it empowers us to go where we've never gone before. That is what leadership is all about. Leaders inspire us to have the courage to take a chance and try something new. They do it without malice and without motivations that are not pure. I believe Howard's motivation is truly to help others. It's a byproduct of making us laugh. This is a byproduct of getting us to open up about our lives, our reality, our humanness. This is a byproduct of his Magic Dust — his creativity, curiosity, passion, and drive to make this a better planet.

HOMEWORK

1. Ask for feedback from five to ten people who work for you. Ask them to answer these questions about you:

   What are my strengths?

What do you think I need to develop to become a stronger leader?

If you could give me any advice, what would it be?

2. If they have time, ask them to rate you from 1 (needing help) to 5 (very strong) on each of the twelve COMPASS areas.

12
Inspiration

For a while now, our team members at PeopleTek have been having a good argument. Does inspiration come from inside us, or is it externally motivated? Many feel you must first go inside to see what you like and what you don't like in order to be inspired. Great leaders are able to see those things within us and light a spark.

It is estimated that only 30 percent of the workforce is engaged. This means that 70 percent are "quiet quitting" — merely showing up, biding their time for other opportunities, or are actively disengaged.

John Quincy Adams said if your actions inspire others to dream more, learn more, and become more, you are a leader.

In a recent call I facilitated, a colleague executive coach asked: which is most important — inspiration or motivation? He proceeded to say that motivation comes from our internal wiring, and inspiration comes from the external environment and other people. I think this idea is worthy of discussion and understanding because it ties to everything we do.

No one can make you do anything. I cannot make you become a better leader. Only you can do that.

So it gets back to a decision you must make on your own. Are you ready to be a leader? Have you decided you want to be a better leader? Have you decided to do the work necessary to become better? Once you've motivated yourself to make this decision, you can begin the process to build your skills, abilities, and talent to become better.

Now, can others inspire you to do more?

QwikCoach[4] content says, "Leaders who are energizing show enthusiasm for what they are doing in ways that raise the energy level of those around them."

---

[4] QwikCoach (a product by E-Coach and Associates)

Ask yourself:

- How passionate or energized am I about achieving goals, maintaining focus, and committing to things that need to be done?
- Am I engaged and involved in my work environment, and do I help others stay engaged, passionate, and challenged when it comes to what is required of them?
- Am I getting others to be motivated and inspired? Do I understand their interests and passions?

First and foremost, ask yourself why you are not engaged.

- Are you doing a job or role that is outside of your life's ambitions? If so, why?
- Are you having personal problems in other areas of your life, such as drinking, gambling, or sex?

Again, only you can give yourself the motivation to address these concerns.

Years ago, I had some personal issues that were affecting my performance and engagement, as I was behaving in ways that weren't serving me well. I didn't realize they were problems until I started seeing a psychologist. He said, "Mike, I am sorry what you're doing is not working." He had me read a few books, and there I discovered what was getting in my way.

It is up to each of us to determine what is getting in our way. A friend of mine recently said his attention was waning with his business. I asked him to write in a log every time he thought he didn't want to be engaged. He said that was too much work. There is an answer for each of you to the question of whether you are engaged or not. Only you know what work you are willing to put in. What amount of time do you wish to invest in yourself? What amount of energy do you want to put in to your career and to be a better leader?

I wish I had the silver bullet for this solution, but then we wouldn't all have free will. It is up to each of us to decide what we want and what we are willing to do to get it.

Sometimes also knowing what we do best gives us the encouragement and self-inspiration to keep moving forward with what we love. If you know the role you most like to play on a team or with others, we've found this knowledge to be helpful. For example, if the role links to your Magic Dust and is something that comes easily, then you are more likely to want to keep doing it. One of my close family members said they want to do only their Magic Dust and nothing else. They are very good at ideas and creativity but not as good at carrying ideas out. The fact is that teams run better and more productively when individuals on the team are doing what they do best. This family member surrounds themselves with many others who are better at finding gaps in the idea and others who get it ready to be launched, then others who carry it out. If they were to perform all roles, then the idea may never get carried out.

WHY HOWARD?

Howard proves my point that all of us are leaders.

Howard is a master at inspiration and motivation. He inspires and motivates by asking the right questions and allowing each of us to be ourselves and to be proud of it.

I'm again reminded of the woman who called in who was 67 years old. She said she had a comedy routine that she wanted

Howard to hear. He said he'd be pleased to hear it. But then he said there was one thing he wanted her to remember: if he was honest and gave her bad feedback, he didn't want her to ever give up on her comedy. He said he was told he was a horrible comedian and that he would never make it. If he had given up because he was not inspired or motivated enough, then we would not be hearing such a wonderful show today — and all the years of joy for himself, his team, and the world would be lost.

What can give us more inspiration than that? Howard is giving us permission to try and fail and keep going no matter who disapproves of us. That proves the point that inspiration and motivation must come internally at some point.

Here is where we apply our key word CourageAbility. This is the art and science of living our lives with courage. To live passionately and with inspiration, we must go inside ourselves. We must empower ourselves to go where we wouldn't without that extra nudge. We can be inspired by others to do it, but at the end of the day it is our responsibility to take that first step and the next several steps.

The reason for a book about Howard is to help everyone benefit from someone who is down to earth, real, innovative, passionate, motivating, a coach, an inspiration, and most of all a dynamite business person. All of it includes a ton of fun. Why can't we have fun with our nuances? If anything, Howard is vulnerable himself and coaches his team to be. They don't always like it, but they know it's important to Howard, the show, and listeners. I don't care what you call it — Howard deserves the credit for leading a team, building an empire, helping people educate the world (or at least those who really listen), and most of all having fun and making people happy with laughter.

He is clear with his vision for excellence, his ability to build a team (rarely do his members leave), his ability to be focused and committed to goals and results. Most important, he is not at all afraid of feedback, to discuss anyone's behavior, including his own, on the radio. This is powerful. If any of you have read *The Five Dysfunctions of a Team*, you'll see that Howard has mastered all solutions offered by the author, Patrick Lencioni.

Having fun, being joyful, being better people, and being able to laugh is an inspiration for all of us. Howard and his team drive these ideas daily in their show. His inspiration to make us laugh drives our behavior to show up and listen. His team's ability to go where they are led drives our behavior to dial in.

I wanted to write about someone controversial who I feel leads in all of the twelve areas of development outlined in our Leadership Journey Program. The reason I chose Howard is that, too often, people have a certain view of what a leader should be. How they should show up. That they are business people who are all buttoned down in expecting how a leader should dress, act, speak, and behave. I wanted to write about someone who leads a team. I wanted to write about someone who empowers us to be better, based on their own actions. I wanted to write about someone who also, based on his behavior, proves that innately we are all leaders.

We lead based on our behaviors. Howard not only points this out with his team, but he also shows us daily that, within ourselves, we are all leaders. We are doing this with behavior that is either helping ourselves and others or hurting ourselves and others. Because we have the power of awareness, we are always a benefit to ourselves and others. We may not realize this reality at the time. By becoming more aware, we realize the powerful impact we can have on ourselves and others. Howard and his team point this out over and over again.

As author Paul Hedderman says, we are way more powerful as individuals than we will ever know. We are the entire ocean. Not just a single wave — the entire ocean! Howard demonstrates the importance of all people on every show. He creates an atmosphere of importance with his team, the audience, his guests, vendors, and superiors. He points out the power we have and that we often forget we have it.

HOMEWORK

1. Complete the homework from Chapter 9: Influence. I think when you do these activities, you will be an inspiration to yourself and others.

13
Continual Learning

Continual learning is the essence of all leadership growth. There are many reasons for this, but here are a few. As we've seen throughout this book, the twelve points of the COMPASS are not easily applied and need refinement and practice for us to be great leaders. As we measure our success, we can determine if we are getting better or worse at the various skills in the COMPASS. This tool provides our purpose and reason for being on the planet. It helps us learn and grow to be better while we are alive. It establishes our destiny. It allows us to contribute to the human experience. It makes us responsible and accountable to leave this place a little better than we found it. Can you imagine if the person who created toilet paper had never had that vision? He helped us all with his vision. Why can't we help others with ours?

We cannot begin to think we know it all, no matter how naturally leadership might have come to us. For example, some say that we are born leaders, and there is no way to improve leadership ability throughout our lives. We are who we are, and that's it. I say that is a misguided approach to life. The PeopleTek team and I live by the premise that we are all leaders, and we can each improve our skills in fundamental areas. Just like in sports — not all of us will be Super Bowl winners. In the 30-plus years we've been developing, there has always been work to do and ways the leader we're coaching can improve. In addition, every leader we've met has awesome Magic Dust. They may not know what it is; but even if they do, there are times they are overusing it and may not be aware. If we are continual learners, then our leadership gap is smaller than for those who are not practicing continual learning.

Let me give an analogy of going to a gym to build our muscles. We hire an awesome trainer. In my case, Duane. I went to Duane for a CrossFit program in 2014. He said, "Let me watch you do some exercises." They consisted of stretching and doing some pushups, sit-ups, and squats. Then a few days later, Duane added lunges and a few days later pull-ups, kettle bells, dumbbells … Eventually I was doing the Workout of the Day.

Now, six years later, we are still mixing and matching exercises. We do a little more each day.

Leadership Learning and developing our self-awareness, relationships, vision, mission, conflict, influencing, and inspiration — all of these muscles take time to build and need attention in specific areas. We must take action and show up at the Leadership Gym, or our muscles will not develop.

These exercises are based on *PeopleTek's Leadership Journey I* and *II* by Michael Kublin and *12 Steps of Courageous Leadership* by Jan Mayer-Rodriguez and Michael Kublin.

Self-awareness is a lifelong process. It means being in tune with yourself and others. Everything starts with your vision, mission, goals, and measures — and the Magic Dust you will use to make them come alive. As a Continual Leadership Learner, you will never give up. You will keep learning, growing, and transforming your behavior and processes to ensure you will be successful. The constant awareness and observations of the behavior of ourselves and others is the Journey. The Journey of living this with full awareness and discovering what you learned along the way.

Self-awareness also requires us to slow down and listen to ourselves and others. Do we have to accept what they tell us? No. However, if we are continually trying to accomplish our goals to be a better leader, then we will realize that we must have a process to measure ourselves and look at our habits, our life plan, our work plan, and how we are showing up in achieving our results.

How do we listen? Do we gather data to enable us to make better decisions on how we are approaching things?

Salespeople do this all the time as they must tweak their approach. Why would we think as leaders of others that we don't need to do the same?

There are listening tools that can help us. I would recommend doing free online tests to measure your listening skills.

Once we have a process to receive feedback, we can then use tools and techniques to sharpen ourselves and how we achieve our goals.

If our goals are not clearly defined, then we need to know that and begin a process to make them clearer. This is the practice I've referred to. You can take any area on the COMPASS and begin exercises to refine your skills in those areas.

Let's go to another example: vision, mission, goals, measures = behavior.

If we have a document that speaks to each of these areas, that is a first step. If we don't have a document, we need to build one. It's just like building leg muscles. You need a base, and then you can work from there. Get out a piece of paper and write something down. Once there, you can give yourself feedback or get it from any number of people mentioned above to find out how you're doing. If you need to refine the document, use that same exercise.

Once we have our documents for vision, mission, goals, measures, and behaviors, the task becomes to complete actions to meet our goals. What are these actions? What are our target dates for action? How do we stop procrastination? Are we making progress?

Let me ask again: where is your vision, mission, goals, and measures document? Where is your action list?

I have a good friend who recommends making five sales calls per day. These are actions. Do you have a list of actions? If not, start one.

Your actions at this point are clear.

1. Take the COMPASS and measure yourself in each of the twelve areas.

2. Begin to document and learn about yourself in each area.

3. Take one area per month for the next year and focus on that.

WHY HOWARD?

Howard is a master at Continual Leadership Learning. He has a counselor whom he works with. He is not afraid to talk about his therapy. He opens up during the calls on his show. He self-reflects about what he's thinking, feeling, and doing — not only with regard to himself but to others as well. How he does this is unique. He uses the show to share his vulnerabilities, what he wants from the staff, what he wants to deliver, and most importantly, his guests' vulnerabilities, goals, and aspirations. His vulnerabilities include his OCD behavior and his need for open discussion of sexuality. He sees what is hidden and exposes the hidden self for himself and his team. And he does this over the radio waves. This is brilliant, and he hides nothing. Being so open is the most effective way for a leader to build trust and understanding, and it's the most critical aspect of any team.

Effective leaders are not afraid of telling the truth — sharing their life, their vision, their dreams and passions. From what we've found over the years in company cultures that are toxic, bad leaders run and hide whenever confronted with a personal question. They don't share, and people are afraid to speak up. Even though everyone is thinking something, no one says it out loud. Howard not only reveals, he asks. He asks everyone what is going on with them personally, and yes, sexually, and he is not afraid to push the envelope. The great thing is he does it in a healthy, honoring, and respectful manner.

Everyone understands what he wants, his expectations, his vision, his goals. Each person is permitted to share theirs as well. Being clear with your vision, mission, goals, and the behaviors you are expecting is so very important for all leaders.

Howard is also unafraid to tell you he sees a psychologist. In therapy, he learns about himself. He applies what he has learned in his daily life. He talks about this openly on the radio for all of us to benefit from his experience of continual learning. He brings up others and their experiences of learning. His recent book *Howard Stern Comes Again* is all about how Howard has learned and grown over the years, and how he has adjusted his style of interviewing, and how he treats his guests. He has spoken about it on the show. He admitted he could change his approach from his earlier days and still get awesome interviews — without being obnoxious and hurting others.

HOMEWORK

Your homework is to go back to each of the areas of the COMPASS and begin to live them fully and passionately every day. Feel free to reach out to me with any questions, any time, at MKublin@peopletekcoaching.com

14
Action Steps

In this chapter, I'll give you some questions to ask yourself regarding continual learning. I think it would be great to pretend you are being interviewed by Howard on the *Howard Stern Show:*

Question 1: Self-Awareness — What have you done recently that shows you how you show up to others? What tools, if any, have you used to learn more about yourself? Have you done a 360 feedback process? Have you done Gallup's StrengthsFinder, DiSC, Myers-Briggs, counseling, or other assessments?

Question 2: Magic Dust — This refers to the skills, abilities, and talents of yourself and all others on your team. Exercise: Do you know what they are? Do you know what happens when they are overused by you and others on your team?

Do you recognize others' Magic Dust and how it helps you, or could help you?

If they overuse their Magic Dust, how does it affect you? What happens when you overuse your Magic Dust and they do the same? How does the conversation go? Do you get anything done?

Question 3: Vision, Mission, Goals, Measures = Behavior — Exercise: What are yours? Does your behavior link up to what you say it is?

In my experience as a coach and leader of PeopleTek, one of the most important elements of being a leader is having a clear vision of what it is you want to accomplish — and also how you're going to get there and be measured. Many leaders work well at managing their teams. They plan, organize, control, and follow up very well. At PeopleTek, our definition of leadership is empowering yourself and others to go where they've never been before and wouldn't go by themselves. This means having direction, purpose, desire. The late, great author of *Think and Grow Rich*, Napoleon Hill, always said that if you have no desire, you won't accomplish much, let alone achieve anything worthwhile.

If you take a look at the formula vision, mission, goals, measures = behaviors, you come out with a specific plan of action. The vision is your dream or aspiration or desire. A vision is very personal, almost impossible, and lives forever. I like to compare it to a telescope. If you've ever looked through a telescope, you can see things way, way out in space. This is a vision; it is difficult for some to see; it is out there, far away, and it has a major purpose for you.

There is no one who displays desire and purpose more than Howard.

In my opinion, by looking at Howard's behavior, we can back into determining his vision, mission, and goals.

We can clearly see he wants to create a world of happiness. He might read this and say, "Oh, really," and probably laugh. I can tell you that his show and the behavior of all on it truly reflect how committed the team is to listeners' enjoyment and laughter.

The mission is the second component of the formula. It signifies a strategy. It is what we are going to do and how we are going to do it. As a symbol for this component, I like to use a pair of binoculars. With binoculars, we bring the vision closer to ourselves. We make it become real for ourselves, our team, and our clients.

In my observation of his behavior, Howard's strategy, again, seems to be his and his entire staff's ability to laugh out loud at themselves. To be vulnerable, to open up. There are no secrets on Howard's show.

In fact, I was thinking if I ever met Howard, how much of my life would I share with him? Would I be open about my wounds from my upbringing?

See, that is what is so great about the formula vision, mission, goals, and measures = behavior. All of us are either leading or just existing. If we are behaving based on a true desire, we are leading. Things are not just happening by mistake; they are developing because of a purpose.

Question 4: Does your team trust you? Exercise: Find out if they do or not by performing an assessment.

Question 5: What is your communication style? Do you understand it, and can you use it for your career? Exercise: Find out your communication style. Find out the styles of the other members of your team. How do they handle conflict, communication, change, decisions, team issues?

Question 6: How does your team measure success? Where are they as a team? What are you doing to lead the team? What results are you having?

Describe the type of conflict you have on the team. Do individuals hold grudges?

Question 7: Describe your team's culture. What values are important there, and what does everyone live by?

Questions 8: Do your team members understand what results are expected for the entire group? Exercise: How do you hold others accountable to results? What are the expectations for results? What happens when results are not achieved?

Question 9: Exercise: If you could change something to make this a better place to work, what would it be? Why? What would benefit us, our team? Is it worth it for everyone and especially our customers?

Question 10: Exercise: How will you practice Continual Leadership Learning? How will you hold yourself accountable?

I believe that Howard should have a leadership academy as part of his show, daily or weekly. This would include one learning event based on the Leadership Journey COMPASS. It would be related to the current day's or week's show and would demonstrate how leadership played a role in that program. For example, Howard interviews someone, and a topic comes up that relates to self-awareness and vulnerability. A discussion with callers is held to debrief how this is leadership, why it is impactful, what could be made better, and how this makes our work environments better and more engaging.

Howard Stern: Setting PeopleTek Standards Since His Beginning

As a conclusion, I would like to share how Howard betters himself and is a Continual Leadership Learner. This book shows you how you can explore learning to be a great leader and build your skills, abilities, and talents, just like Howard is doing now. For example:

Howard betters himself by taking risks. He took risks in his career, while many people, including his family members, said it would be impossible for him to succeed in radio. He never gave up his passion, despite all the blowback from others. I had a similar experience. To this day, I have family members who wonder how I can make a living coaching and developing others. Even writing this book was a challenge — some people walked away from me because I was writing about Howard. As an individual, you need to take risks for yourself and your career. Are you up for the challenge?

Howard betters his staff and team by honoring how special they are. He uses them for their Magic Dust. Robin can be who she is — sensitive but with an edge. Fred is quiet but active in every discussion with his sound antics, and occasionally talks about his quiet weirdness. Gary has his producing, and he shares an enthusiastic way of being. Ronnie can express his odd behavior over sexuality. The list goes on and on through the years.

Howard doesn't back down from his team members, and he seems to believe it's fine to have an argument with each other. He is loyal and has never let a team member go that I know of. PeopleTek has done the same thing with our team. We use our team for their Magic Dust and allow them multiple ways to participate and engage. I encourage you to gain knowledge of your Magic Dust and the Magic Dust of others. Engage others in developing and implementing your vision, mission, goals, and measures.

Howard betters his guests by allowing them to be themselves. He is vulnerable, and this gives permission to his staff, callers, and celebrity guests to be vulnerable. He digs deep into their lives, and that brings out the best in each guest. I've seen him do this in many shows, and he doesn't back down from a deep question. He gets answers. He learned through counseling that he didn't need to be so rough, sarcastic, and insensitive. He could get deep answers by just asking questions in a softer, more caring manner.

Most of us won't ask the deeper questions. Even me, because I did not want to hurt someone's feelings, in the past I have avoided some issues and didn't ask the deeper questions of my colleagues and clients. I am so glad that I built these muscles, as they make for a stronger coach and better relationships and outcomes. What are you afraid to ask of your colleagues, customers, and peers? What is this fear doing to your relationships?

Howard betters all of us as his listeners. Why? Because he is a great listener. He hears the surface message and digs for the deeper message. This gives us, his listeners, permission to do the same. Yes, there are shows that are not worth listening to, but those happen less and less frequently. In each show — even in the clips they post on social media of past shows — Howard gets us to listen because he is not afraid. He gets us to think about ourselves and our relationships. We are all better off because he won't back down, and he gets us to think about how we are showing up as leaders — how we are feeling and thinking and what we are doing to improve. As we listen to Howard, we can't help but reflect on how we can build our communication skills. Are we listening and heeding the message and assisting the speaker? Are we able to be discerning when required about what we are hearing?

IN DOING ALL THE ABOVE, we can see Howard's meaningful work. All of us need to do the actions outlined in the book. When we do, we will become better leaders for ourselves and others. Our behaviors and decisions guiding us to successful outcomes is what we strive for as leaders and business owners — this is the ultimate goal of self-improvement in leadership. Leadership begins with us and starts with doing our inner work and then expands to the teams we lead, our families, communities and ultimately creates progress for everyone. This is all about you, the listener. We all benefit from Howard's hard work. We should always find ways to benefit from the hard work of our leaders.

The path toward my own meaningful work began when I received feedback from my team. That feedback, while it hurt, changed my life in a positive way — not only as a leader of myself but as a leader of others. There would be no leadership program that changed thousands of lives without me having received the feedback that I was visionary, motivating, and inspiring, but I was also wishy-washy and didn't hold others accountable. Through the years, by building skills in the areas of the COMPASS I needed to strengthen, my career and life changed. Now you can change yours too.

My self-confidence was also very low, and I didn't know why. Ultimately, it was because I didn't believe in myself and my Magic Dust. I would not allow myself to be real with everyone. I think this is a process of self-awareness and discovery of what the true messages are that you wish to share with the world. We can easily see it with Howard, and now I believe I am living more in alignment with my authentic self as well. I want the same for all of you reading this book right now.

My communication with others was impacted by being more honest and direct, less fearful about what others think, and more confident in the vision, mission, and goals I established for myself and the team.

And my work expanded to my "listeners" — when I did the podcast *Leadership Is a Process, Not an Event*, I brought in the extraordinary skills, abilities, and talents of others. I am so grateful to be surrounded by a team of executive coaches, people in supporting roles, and customers who eat, sleep, and breathe the challenge of becoming the best they can be — no matter what age or stage they are at in life. Our work in the three areas we've highlighted in the COMPASS never stops. The key is to start. When will you?

This is the path I help people travel. It's important to align yourself with Magic Dust congruency and community, authentic confidence in the face of external or internal conflict, and self-determined awareness and development. Yes, the work is hard, but it's worth it. And if it seems hopeless, I assure you it is not, and I'm confident that I would prove that to you as your coach. I fully recommend working with someone on your leadership and strengths. And I'm up for the challenge. If you need help, that's what I'm here to offer.

When I started in my career, I was not aligned with my Magic Dust — to be a motivator and inspirer who helps leaders, teams, and organizations improve their people skills so they can experience joy and passion every day in their careers.

I had to start with myself. This meant taking a risk by leaving corporate America and starting a leadership company. Little did I know that I would see a series of people just like me — they were good at doing their jobs or tasks, but they were never trained to be the true leaders they had the potential to be. That had to change. That is when I made the move.

What do you need in order to reach your full potential as a leader? To find out, start doing the exercises in this book. If you have trouble, seek out a coach or call or write to us for help.

I want you to start the process today of having the most impact in your life and career. As Dr. Fischler, my great friend who I previously mentioned, told me, he wished he had taken the program when he was 30 years old or younger. I believe we should all do this work outlined in the book as soon as we can start. It's never too early to begin. In doing our self work and using the tools outlined in the book, we all can have more joy and better outcomes with our careers, guiding ourselves and others.

My advice would be to not delay one minute of your development. Start reading and doing the exercises in this book now.

Epilogue

I have this saying: "I want to be physically, mentally, emotionally, spiritually, sexually, financially, and relationally, the healthiest in the cemetery." I can think of no one better who leads this kind of life than Howard. I can't thank him enough. For too long I was afraid of saying what was on my mind or hurting someone's feelings. While this fear helped me get along with others, it hurt me in various areas of my life. Although this is a book about leadership, it is really about life — how we can live better, more fulfilled lives. Howard is a true example of how to do that for everyone to emulate.

It's been a true pleasure listening to his show when I can and laughing out loud in my car. I believe Howard's best is yet to come.

First and foremost, thank you to my children, Jacquelyn and Harrison, who each day teach me more about life and unconditional love and lead me to be a continual learner. Thank you to my late mother, Carol Kublin. Without her endless love and kindness to everyone including me, I wouldn't have had the Magic Dust to have gone into this field in the first place. Thank you to my late father, Alvin Kublin, for his relentless pursuit of business, and later in life peace and happiness. Thank you to my second mom, Phyllis, who taught me many things and helped me to be persistent in going after my goals and to look at things more critically. You both taught me the power of making a decision. Thanks to my late sister, Debbie, who showed me you can step out of the box and still be okay. Thanks to my brother, Brett, who taught me resilience. And of course, I have so much gratitude for my love, Wilda Bello Godinez, and her entire family. Together, we have shared many special moments.

To my friends Steven and Paula Pruett, who have been with me every step of the way in learning about true leadership, I am eternally grateful. At that, there are so many friends, family, clients, and colleagues and awesome PeopleTek Team in my life that I wish to thank personally for helping me with my life, work, and this book. It has been a journey together that has uncovered many of life's treasures for me. I cannot thank each and every one of you enough. You know who you are and, after publishing this book, if I haven't already told you personally, I will again soon.

This book would not have been possible without the help of Rob Kosberg, Bob Harpole, Matt Schnarr, and the Best Seller Publishing team.

Sending endless thanks and hugs to you all!

About the Author

Michael Kublin and his PeopleTek team have been developing leaders, teams, and organizations for over 25 years. With what started as less than exemplary feedback from his staff, Mike ultimately created the Leadership Journey and launched the PeopleTek Coaching Team (www.peopletekcoaching.com). The Leadership Journey is a six-month program led by an Executive Coach who has transformed the skills of many leaders, their teams, and organizations. It's all about how you treat yourself and others. A sponsor for the program called it "the real diversity and inclusion program." Mike's experience leading corporate teams in a large information technology department and a major financial institution provided the background to discover what worked and what didn't to engage people throughout an organization.

Mike is an MCEC Executive Coach in the Association of Corporate Executive Coaches, the author of *PeopleTek's Leadership Journey I* and *II*, and coauthor, with Jan Mayer-Rodriguez, of *12 Steps for Courageous Leadership* and *Leadership Insights*.

Made in the USA
Columbia, SC
04 May 2024